How Serious a Problem Is Computer Hacking?

Patricia D. Netzley

INCONTROVERSY

ReferencePoint
Press®

San Diego, CA

© 2014 ReferencePoint Press, Inc.
Printed in the United States

For more information, contact:
ReferencePoint Press, Inc.
PO Box 27779
San Diego, CA 92198
www.ReferencePointPress.com

LIBRARY OF CONGRESS CATALOGING-IN-PUBLICATION DATA

Netzley, Patricia D.
  How serious a problem is computer hacking? / by Patricia D. Netzley.
    pages cm. -- (In controversy)
  Audience: Grade 9 to 12
  Includes bibliographical references and index.
    ISBN-13: 978-1-60152-550-5 (hardback) -- ISBN-10: 1-60152-550-8 (hardback)
  1. Computer hackers--Juvenile literature. 2. Computer crimes--Juvenile literature. 3. Computer security--Juvenile literature. I. Title.
    HV6773.N47395   2013
    364.16'8--dc23
                                                           2013014096

Contents

Foreword

In 2008, as the US economy and economies worldwide were falling into the worst recession since the Great Depression, most Americans had difficulty comprehending the complexity, magnitude, and scope of what was happening. As is often the case with a complex, controversial issue such as this historic global economic recession, looking at the problem as a whole can be overwhelming and often does not lead to understanding. One way to better comprehend such a large issue or event is to break it into smaller parts. The intricacies of global economic recession may be difficult to understand, but one can gain insight by instead beginning with an individual contributing factor, such as the real estate market. When examined through a narrower lens, complex issues become clearer and easier to evaluate.

This is the idea behind ReferencePoint Press's *In Controversy* series. The series examines the complex, controversial issues of the day by breaking them into smaller pieces. Rather than looking at the stem cell research debate as a whole, a title would examine an important aspect of the debate such as *Is Stem Cell Research Necessary?* or *Is Embryonic Stem Cell Research Ethical?* By studying the central issues of the debate individually, researchers gain a more solid and focused understanding of the topic as a whole.

Each book in the series provides a clear, insightful discussion of the issues, integrating facts and a variety of contrasting opinions for a solid, balanced perspective. Personal accounts and direct quotes from academic and professional experts, advocacy groups, politicians, and others enhance the narrative. Sidebars add depth to the discussion by expanding on important ideas and events. For quick reference, a list of key facts concludes every chapter. Source notes, an annotated organizations list, bibliography, and index provide student researchers with additional tools for papers and class discussion.

The *In Controversy* series also challenges students to think critically about issues, to improve their problem-solving skills, and to sharpen their ability to form educated opinions. As President Barack Obama stated in a March 2009 speech, success in the twenty-first century will not be measurable merely by students' ability to "fill in a bubble on a test but whether they possess 21st century skills like problem-solving and critical thinking and entrepreneurship and creativity." Those who possess these skills will have a strong foundation for whatever lies ahead.

No one can know for certain what sort of world awaits today's students. What we can assume, however, is that those who are inquisitive about a wide range of issues; open-minded to divergent views; aware of bias and opinion; and able to reason, reflect, and reconsider will be best prepared for the future. As the international development organization Oxfam notes, "Today's young people will grow up to be the citizens of the future: but what that future holds for them is uncertain. We can be quite confident, however, that they will be faced with decisions about a wide range of issues on which people have differing, contradictory views. If they are to develop as global citizens all young people should have the opportunity to engage with these controversial issues."

In Controversy helps today's students better prepare for tomorrow. An understanding of the complex issues that drive our world and the ability to think critically about them are essential components of contributing, competing, and succeeding in the twenty-first century.

Hacking as Cybercrime

In October 2012 the US Secret Service notified the state of South Carolina that someone had broken through the security protections of the computer system used by the state's revenue department. This case of computer hacking—whereby someone without authorization gains access to the software, files, and other aspects of a computer system—came to light after the thief, who was located outside of the country, got into the computer's database. By doing so, the hacker was able to steal 4 million Social Security numbers as well as bank account information from state taxpayers and businesses. This data would enable the hacker to steal money from individuals whose records were in the system.

A few days later the first victims of this crime appeared. Among them was a South Carolina couple, Tina and Wade Mathers, who owned a small catering company. Their bank account was drained of $4,000 as a result of the breach of security. "It was very surprising when we get up one morning and found thousands of dollars missing from our account and that's when the reality really set in, like, oh my goodness, this is not going to be good,"[1] said Wade Mathers.

However, the hacker did not take all the money in one transaction. Instead, the thief made ten withdrawals from the Mathers's bank account over two days. The hacker also took precautions to make it harder for authorities to track the requests for the transfers back to their source, using false computer identification methods and rerouting the money from one computer system to another. None of these transactions or any others connected to the South Carolina hacking have yet been connected to the culprit. In fact, the couple may never get their money back. Consequently, Tina Mathers says that the state officials who failed to protect their computer system "need to educate everyone on exactly what's happened, take responsibility for what's happened and then help those of us who are truly victims of this situation."[2]

Old Systems

It is not unusual that South Carolina did not detect the crime on its own. The FBI estimates that for every company that knows it has been hacked, one hundred others are unaware that they have been the victim of this kind of cybercrime. Part of the problem is that many companies and government agencies have not upgraded their technology to keep pace with today's cybercriminals. Internet security expert Brendan Hannigan reports:

> Organizations can't just rely on the traditional tools of the past to make sure the data they're collecting and exposing to the Internet is protected. Smart cyber criminals can skirt around these older defensive technologies and blend into the background noise of an organization's operations. They're skilled and patient enough to do reconnaissance of an organization's [computer] network over months or years, waiting for just the right chance to steal sensitive information.[3]

Because of such persistence, many computer users have suffered a cyberattack. Internet security experts stated in February 2013 that three out of four Americans have fallen victim to cybercrime as a direct result of being hacked, and 90 percent of businesses had been victimized by a hacker over the previous twelve months. In some cases the victim lost all the data stored on the hacked computer, thereby compounding the harm of the cyberattack.

Also compounding the harm is the fact that sometimes a hacking leaves computers, computer systems, or websites unusable. In such cases a business that depends on Internet transactions can lose a significant amount of money. According to Richard Power,

> "Organizations can't just rely on the traditional tools of the past to make sure the data they're collecting and exposing to the Internet is protected."[3]

— Internet security expert Brendan Hannigan.

Although not all hackers are criminals, hacking attacks that aim to disrupt service or steal information or money have become increasingly common. Individuals, businesses, and even governments are at risk.

editorial director of the Computer Security Institute, just one case of hacking can cost an online business $600,000 to $7 million a day, depending on the company's revenues, as well as the monetary value of lost employee time. Businesses can also lose money when hackers wipe out important information needed to run the business and/or to manufacture products.

Black, White, and Gray Hats

However, security experts note that not all hackers are criminals. According to hacking terminology, hackers fall into three broad groups: black hats, white hats, and gray hats. Criminals are a type of black hat, someone who hacks for selfish and harmful reasons. These reasons might be to steal money, to enact revenge on someone, or to perpetrate malicious pranks. In contrast, white hats hack in order to be helpful. For example, they might want to test a computer system for security threats so they can notify users to take steps to protect the system. Gray hats hack for what they believe are noble purposes, although not everyone agrees with their beliefs.

Gray hats who are motivated by a desire to effect political or social change are commonly known as hacktivists. Some hacktivists, for example, have broken into computer systems in order to bring to light certain government actions that they believe are wrong. Others have hacked in order to provide the public with restricted information that the hacker thinks should be available to everyone without cost.

However, hacktivists have also released the private information of individuals, such as phone numbers and addresses, in ways that cause these people personal harm. One former member of a hacktivist group called Anonymous says this kind of damage is the reason he left the group. He complains that an offshoot of the group, called AntiSec, "released gig after gig of innocent people's information. For what? What did they do? Does Anon [Anonymous] have the right to remove the anonymity of innocent people? They are always talking about people's right to remain anonymous so why are they removing that right?"[4]

According to a Verizon report on data breaches, in 2011 hacktivists were responsible for 100 million of the 174 million records stolen from computer systems that year. However, this data was taken from only a few sources, so as Peter Ludlow of the *New York Times* points out, "this means that in 2011 if you were worried about an intrusion into your system it was 33 times more likely that the perpetrator would be a criminal, nation state or disgruntled employee than a hacktivist."[5] In other words, most hackers are black hats, not gray hats.

Harmful Attacks

But regardless of motivation, hackers can use various methods to affect how a computer, computer system, or network operates.

One of the most common is to give the target computer a virus, a self-replicating program that changes the way the computer operates and can spread from computer to computer like a disease. Employed by malicious pranksters or people seeking revenge, viruses can wipe out data and make a computer unusable. Viruses spread through e-mails can also install a backdoor program on a machine that enables the hacker to do further damage later, particularly by providing a way to smuggle other programs into the computer. Such programs can allow hackers to access, delete, edit, or otherwise corrupt computer files. They can also be used to steal passwords and credit card information, to monitor what is being typed on a keyboard, or to spy on video or audio conversations.

To prevent such activities, many computer users turn to experts in the computer security industry, and because cybercrime is growing, this industry is growing as well. In 2012, according to the research firm International Data Corporation, big companies spent roughly 9 percent more on computer security over the previous year, at an estimated cost of more than $32 billion. Consequently, investors have poured money into creating new computer security companies. For example, according to a report compiled by the accounting firm PricewaterhouseCoopers and the National Venture Capital Association, which represents investment companies, in 2011 investors provided $935 million in capital to tech security companies, which was double the amount invested in such companies in 2010.

"Security is a growing market and it will grow forever."[6]

— Computer security investment partner Ray Rothrock.

However, experts note that as the number and sophistication of computer security companies have increased, so too have hackers become more numerous and more sophisticated. Hackers have also sent investors in computer security companies threatening e-mails and have launched cyberattacks against computer security companies in an attempt to shut them down. Nonetheless, as computer security investment partner Ray Rothrock notes, "security is a growing market and it will grow forever,"[6] because individuals, businesses, and government agencies will always have a need to protect themselves against hackers.

Facts

- In 2011, 77 million Sony PlayStation accounts were hacked at once, successfully providing the hackers with users' personal data.

- Internet security company webyFly reports that in 2012 roughly $1 trillion worth of intellectual property was stolen via hacking.

- According to a study by the University of Maryland, weak passwords result in 2,244 hacking attacks per day.

- According to a 2012 report by security software corporation Symantec on Internet security threats, in 2011 more than 232.4 million identities were exposed worldwide, mainly as part of hacking attacks designed to acquire customer-related information.

- Verizon Business reports that in 2012, 79 percent of hacking victims were targets of opportunity rather than preplanned targets, and 96 percent of hacking attacks were fairly easy for hackers to accomplish.

What Are the Origins of the Problem of Hacking?

In the 1980s a popular computer word-processing program called Scribe allowed users to try out the software for free for ninety days. At that point it would stop working, and users would have to pay a fee to reactivate the software. Every year thereafter, the software would do the same thing, requiring another payment in order to keep the program operational. In addition, some copies of the user's software would shut down even though reactivation payment was not yet due.

Known as a time bomb, this shutdown feature was put into Scribe by the software's developer, computer scientist Brian Reid, after he sold the rights to Scribe to computer software company Unilogic. Reid had no compunctions about creating something that would ensure people would have to keep paying to use what was now Unilogic's software. However, other computer software experts were dismayed at the idea of coupling computer use with monthly fees, and many believed that software should either be free to all or a one-time purchase.

One of Reid's harshest critics was Richard Stallman, who founded a free-software movement to fight the use of time bombs, such as Scribe's, and other restrictions on computer access. Stallman developed his belief in free software first while a graduate student and later as a computer programmer at the Massachusetts Institute of Technology (MIT). In discussing how his time there influenced his beliefs, Stallman says:

> I went to MIT in 1971, and I became part of a community of people who shared software. This community went all the way back to the beginning of computation. It included various high-powered computer science departments, and sometimes computer companies—people who would write programs and share them with the whole community, and people would improve them. In fact, at MIT we entirely used software that was part of this community. We did not make big fuss over whether it was free, but if anyone wanted a copy, they could have it.[7]

Making Things Work Better

Members of this MIT hacker community, which arose in the late 1950s and continued throughout the 1980s, shared information because they believed that only through cooperation could computer software be made better, and improving performance was their main focus. In fact, one story for the origin of the word *hacker* is that the first computer experts at MIT borrowed it from members of a model train group at the institute who used the term *hacking* to refer to their attempts to improve the performance of their electric trains, tracks, and switches. These train hackers apparently started using the word because to hack at something meant to whittle away at it, a concept they connected to the way they tried to solve problems.

Early hackers were typically motivated by a desire to do whatever it took to make computers perform better. Sometimes, however, this desire caused them to do things that others might consider unethical. For example, one hacker might use another hacker's idea without giving that person credit. Consequently, the hacker community had many discussions about whether the individual or the hack is more important, and such discussions led to an unwritten code of ethics that guided the behavior of hackers not just at

Richard Stallman, pictured in 1998, founded a free-software movement to fight restricted access to computer technology. He believed that such technology should be shared with the broader community so that it could be improved and used by all who wished to use it.

MIT but elsewhere. The code emphasizes being selfless instead of selfish, doing things for the good of the computer rather than for the good of the computer programmer. Stallman explains, "The hacker ethic refers to the feelings of right and wrong, to the ethical ideas this community of people had—that knowledge should be shared with other people who can benefit from it, and that important resources should be utilized rather than wasted."[8]

But Stallman adds that not all hackers worry about ethics. He says, "Just because someone enjoys hacking does not mean he has an ethical commitment to treating other people properly. Some hackers care about ethics—I do, for instance—but that is not part of being a hacker, it is a separate trait. Some stamp collectors care a lot about ethics, while other stamp collectors don't. It is the same for hackers."[9]

Moreover, even among those early hackers who adhered to the code of ethics, notions of what constituted right and wrong were not always in sync with the morals of society as a whole. Many of the first hackers thought nothing of breaking rules. Stallman reports that at MIT, "Hackers never had much respect for bureaucratic restrictions. If the computer was sitting idle because the administrators wouldn't let them use it, they would sometimes figure out how to bypass the obstacles and use it anyway. If this required cleverness, it would be fun in itself, as well as making it possible to do other hacking (for instance, useful work) on the computer instead of twiddling one's thumbs."[10]

Pranks

Many of the first hacks were actually pranks. In fact, what most experts believe to be the first computer virus ever to infect computers among the general public was created as a practical joke. Called Elk Cloner, it began to spread in 1982 because of Richard Skrenta, a ninth grader at St. Lebanon Senior High School near Pittsburgh, Pennsylvania. Skrenta had previously pranked his friends by giving them disks of computer games that he had copied himself and then altered so that they would display a funny message before game play could begin. However, some of his friends responded by refusing to accept any more disks from him, and he found this frustrating.

Consequently, during his 1981 winter break from school, he spent his time working with his Apple II computer to come up with a way to continue the prank that ultimately made him famous. "It was some dumb little practical joke," Skrenta, now in his late forties and an accomplished computer programmer, says. "I guess if you had to pick between being known for this and not being known for anything, I'd rather be known for this."[11]

Skrenta figured out how to put a code on a disk that would automatically copy itself from the disk into the computer's memory after the disk was inserted and the computer was started, or booted up. Known today as a boot-sector virus, this code could then copy itself onto other disks put into the machine. This meant, for ex-

"The hacker ethic refers to the feelings of right and wrong, to the ethical ideas this community of people had—that knowledge should be shared with other people who can benefit from it, and that important resources should be utilized rather than wasted."[8]

— Richard Stallman, computer programmer and founder of a freesoftware movement.

Time Bombs

A time bomb is a set of instructions secretly placed within a computer program and designed to activate on a specific date. One of the most famous time bombs went off at a Volga automobile plant in the Soviet Union in 1986. Placed in the plant's computer system by a disgruntled employee, it was timed to stop all production on the main assembly line for a day, a week after the employee, a computer programmer, had left on vacation. The incident gained notoriety because it was the first hacking case to be tried in the Soviet Union. The hacker was convicted, sentenced to three years in jail, and prohibited from ever again working as a computer programmer. The jail sentence was suspended.

ample, that if someone used an infected computer to put files on a new disk and then gave that disk to a friend to use, the friend's computer would soon be infected as well.

The result of the infection would not be apparent at first. Skrenta's code would wait until an infected disk had been booted up forty-nine times, and on the fiftieth time it would display a taunting poem, titled "Elk Cloner," that claimed that the Cloner would infiltrate computers, modify them, and prove impossible to get rid of. In fact, this is what happened. While Skrenta's first victims were friends from his community, years later he would hear stories of computers being infected in other parts of the world. For example, in the 1990s a sailor stationed in the Middle East during the first Gulf War encountered the virus on his Apple computer.

Turning Destructive

Another boot-sector virus targeted computers running the Microsoft operating system beginning in 1986. Like Elk Cloner, it displayed a message, but in this case the screen also showed the phone number of the computer repair shop owned by two brothers in Pakistan who created the virus. When confronted about their creation, the two said that they had devised the virus as a way to punish people who were copying software illegally. However, except for the message, the virus did not do any significant damage to infected computers.

Soon, however, other viruses appeared that were not so harmless. For example, in 1987 a virus began attacking IBM personal computers at Lehigh University in Bethlehem, Pennsylvania. Called the Lehigh virus, it was the first virus to attack files stored on a computer's hard drive, although it worked in much the same way as Elk Cloner. That is, the Lehigh virus infected a computer's operating system, copied itself onto a disk that had been inserted into the machine, and then traveled on that disk to other computers. However, in this case the virus was programmed to wipe out all the data on the afflicted computer after it had infected four disks.

Phreaking

In the 1980s hackers also increasingly put their efforts into finding ways to steal phone services via hacking. Phone hacking—commonly known as phreaking—initially referred simply to a practice whereby hackers broke into regional and international phone networks in order to make free calls. The phone system was important to early phreakers because at the time, computers went online via a dial-up system that used a modem to access the Internet through a phone line.

One of the first phreakers was John Draper, also known as Captain Crunch, who gained notoriety in 1971 after *Esquire* magazine wrote about his activities. Draper used a whistle given away free in a Cap'n Crunch cereal box to duplicate a tone recognized by the AT&T phone system as the signal that a phone line was available and open to place a new call. He had first heard about this tone from a blind boy who often whistled up his own free calls, but Draper soon provided a way to make phreaking even easier. He built electronic devices, commonly referred to as blue boxes, that could emit various tones that would affect phone systems in other ways related to routing calls.

But Draper's reasons for getting into phreaking were more about computer hacking than about making free calls. Using the pseudonym Captain Crunch, he told Ron Rosenbaum, the reporter for *Esquire*:

Ma Bell [slang for the phone company] is a system I want to explore. It's a beautiful system, you know, but Ma Bell

White Hats or Black Hats?

Sometimes the hackers behind a seemingly harmful cyberattack claim that their motives were good. This was the case when a group calling itself the Unknowns hacked several prominent websites, including those of NASA and the US Air Force, in May 2012. Although the group subsequently released confidential data found on those websites, it also insisted it was merely trying to expose security risks so the websites could be fixed. The Unknowns explained, "We probably harmed you a bit but that's not really our goal because if it was then all of your websites would be completely defaced, but we know that within a week or two the vulnerabilities we found will be patched and that's what we're actually looking for." They also said, "We can't call ourselves White Hat Hackers but we're not Black Hat Hackers either."

Security expert Brian Royer and others suggest that the hackers were simply trying to prove they can make private information public. Royer says, "So the takeaway is the Unknowns are completely on the up-and-up and we should trust them because they're not like the others, right? Nope—not buying it. . . . Sounds like classic, old-school hacking to me."

Quoted in Jason Ryan, "NASA, Air Force and Harvard Computers Hacked by 'The Unknowns,'" *National Security* (blog), ABC News, May 4, 2012. http://abcnews.go.com.

Brian Royer, "Where in Hacking the Ends Justify the Means," *SophosLabs Insights* (blog), Dark Reading, May 8, 2012. www.darkreading.com.

screwed up. . . . I learned how she screwed up from a couple of blind kids who wanted me to build a device. A certain device. They said it could make free calls. I wasn't interested in free calls. But when these blind kids told me I could make calls into a computer, my eyes lit up. I wanted to learn about computers. I wanted to learn about Ma Bell's computers. So I built the little device.[12]

Soon other people began building and selling blue boxes, and their use spread. The majority of phreakers used them simply to make free phone calls, but like Captain Crunch some used them to hack into computers that were online. In telling how one phreaker, Al Gilbertson (not his real name), got into this activity, Rosenbaum reports:

He began playing with computers in earnest when he learned he could use his blue box in tandem with the computer terminal installed in his apartment by the instrumentation firm he worked for. The printout terminal and keyboard were equipped with acoustical coupling, so that by coupling his little ivory Princess phone to the terminal and then coupling his blue box on that, he could M-F [multifrequency tone] his way into other computers with complete anonymity, and without charge; program and re-program them at will; feed them false or misleading information; tap and steal from them. He explained to me that he taps computers by busying out all the lines, then going into a verification trunk, listening into the passwords and instructions one of the time sharers uses, and . . . imitating them.[13]

Some phreakers used their access to the phone system primarily to engage in mischief. For example, one arbitrarily disconnected the phones of celebrities, while another intentionally crashed a phone system. But other phreakers stole not just services from phone companies but money from individuals. For example, one phreaker used a phone company's digital switchboard system to scam people via money wiring. Others stole and used the numbers of phone calling cards (a type of credit card) from phone company computer systems, which meant that their calls were being paid for by the individuals to whom the cards had been issued.

Law Enforcement Efforts

Much of the information obtained through phreaking, including the stolen calling card numbers and the methods used to tamper with phone and computer systems, was shared on computer bulletin board systems (also known as BBS). People who connected, or logged in, to bulletin board systems could share software and information with other users via downloading, uploading, exchanging e-mails, chatting, and communicating through message boards. As the number of bulletin board systems devoted to disseminating information on illegal phreaking activities grew, phone companies began calling on the federal government to step in to end the phreaking. In addition, lawmakers in the United States and the United Kingdom passed legislation to make it easier to prosecute people who used computers to engage in illegal activities. Members of law enforcement also started working to combat this kind of crime.

One of the largest federal antihacking efforts was Operation Sundevil, named for a football stadium in Arizona that was near the operation's temporary headquarters. The two-year investigation was followed by a three-day period of arrests in May 1990. Overall, the operation involved more than 150 Secret Service agents, typically accompanied by local and/or state police, to raid locations—most of them private homes—in more than a dozen cities across the country. They confiscated roughly forty-two computer systems, about twenty-five of which were running bulletin board systems that were then shut down, as well as roughly twenty-three thousand computer disks. These disks were later found to contain pirated computer games (games that have been illegally copied and distributed), stolen computer codes and credit card numbers, and other illegal material that had been shared on bulletin board systems.

Many of those involved in these activities were young men still

"Our experience shows that many computer hacker suspects are no longer misguided teenagers mischievously playing games with their computers in their bedrooms. Some are now high tech computer operators using computers to engage in unlawful conduct."[14]

— Garry M. Jenkins of the Secret Service.

in school. Nonetheless, the federal agents involved in Operation Sundevil considered them a serious threat. Garry M. Jenkins, the assistant director of the Secret Service at the time of the raids, said, "Our experience shows that many computer hacker suspects are no longer misguided teenagers mischievously playing games with their computers in their bedrooms. Some are now high tech computer operators using computers to engage in unlawful conduct."[14]

Jenkins also argued that once a hacker started down the wrong path, it could lead to an escalation of illegal activity. He stated:

> Recently, we have witnessed an alarming number of young people who, for a variety of sociological and psychological reasons, have become attached to their computers and are exploiting their potential in a criminal manner. Often, a progression of criminal activity occurs which involves telecommunications fraud (free long distance phone calls), unauthorized access to other computers (whether for profit, fascination, ego, or the intellectual challenge), credit card fraud (cash advances and unauthorized purchases of goods), and then move on to other destructive activities like computer viruses.[15]

Hacking Groups

Nonetheless, only four people were arrested as a result of the raids. In addition, some computer experts estimate that only a tenth of the bulletin board systems then involved in sharing information on illegal hacking activities were shut down as a result of the operation. But the operation was still considered a success because it frightened many in the hacker community into avoiding illegal activities in the future.

This does not mean, however, that the number of cases of illegal hacking dropped significantly. The most devoted hackers continued their activities after Operation Sundevil and subsequent raids. Determined to show that no one could keep them from hacking computers, many of them banded together, united by a common enemy—the government.

One of the most prominent hacker groups was L0pht Heavy Industries, which operated out of the Boston, Massachusetts, area

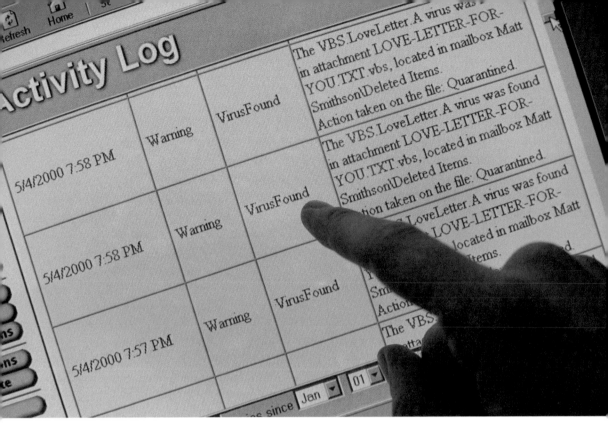

Activity Log

5/4/2000 7:58 PM	Warning	VirusFound	The VBS.LoveLetter.A virus was in attachment LOVE-LETTER-FOR-YOU.TXT.vbs, located in mailbox Matt Smithson\Deleted Items. Action taken on the file: Quarantined.
5/4/2000 7:58 PM	Warning	VirusFound	The VBS.LoveLetter.A virus was found in attachment LOVE-LETTER-FOR-YOU.TXT.vbs, located in mailbox Matt Smithson\Deleted Items. ...tion taken on the file: Quarantined.
5/4/2000 7:57 PM	Warning	VirusFound	...LoveLetter.A virus was found ...LOVE-LETTER-FOR- ...located in mailbox Matt ...Items.

...s since Jan ▼ 01 ▼

A computer user looks through a May 2000 activity log that identifies e-mails with attachments infected by the ILOVEYOU, or LOVE-LETTER, virus. Computer experts estimate that this virus infected 10 percent of all computers connected to the Internet.

from 1992 to 2000. During this period it became a hacker think tank that provided information not only on hacking but also on how to improve computer security, and it gradually moved from black-hat hacking to white-hat hacking. Because of this, seven members of the group were asked to testify before the US Congress in 1998 at a Government Affairs Committee hearing on federal computer security. They stated that it would take them only thirty minutes to shut down the Internet.

But just as some hackers were making the transition from bad acts to good acts, the 1990s and early 2000s also saw a dramatic increase in hacking intended to cause trouble and/or steal money. The efforts of black-hat hackers were aided by the spread of Internet use during this period and the fact that more and more people who were ignorant about computers were communicating by e-mail. E-mails and websites provided relatively easy ways for hackers to gain access to computer systems, to trick people into providing personal data, and to spread computer viruses, especially before people became aware of Internet security issues.

One example of how much damage a hacker could do during this period was the ILOVEYOU virus, which first appeared in May 2000. It was transmitted via an e-mail attachment that appeared to be a love letter. When a recipient opened the attachment, the computer was immediately infected by the virus, which then used the computer's stored list of e-mail contacts to send the virus to others while making the computer inoperable for its user. Computer experts estimate that this virus infected 10 percent of all computers connected to the Internet and cost approximately $5.5 billion in damages.

A Global Problem

Over the next decade viruses continued to plague computer users, and as Internet use grew and spread to all corners of the globe, hacking spread too. In fact, experts noted that whereas hacking was once largely a US activity, in the 2000s an increasing number of hackers were operating outside the United States. Rik Ferguson, senior security researcher at computer security software company Trend Micro, reports that "[hacking] groups emerged around the world in places as far flung as Pakistan and India, where there is fierce competition between the hackers."[16]

Ene, a computer security expert who blogs under a pseudonym for the *TechSentry* blog on hacking-related issues, says that today these international hackers are involved not only in crimes against individuals and businesses but also in hacktivism. He writes, "In Romania groups such as HackersBlog have hit various companies. In China and Russia, many hackers are believed to act as proxies for their governments. In Nigeria a group of hacktivists called 'Naija Hacktivist' also defaced a Nigerian government website in an attempt to make a statement."[17]

While cybercrime continues to rise in the United States, experts note that there has also been a rise in the kind of hacking that was prevalent in the early days of the activity. Cybercrime analyst Brian Krebs says, "It's not too hard to understand why so many people would pay attention to activity that is,

"[Hacking] groups emerged around the world in places as far flung as Pakistan and India, where there is fierce competition between the hackers."[16]

— Rik Ferguson, senior security researcher at computer security software company Trend Micro.

for the most part, old school hacking—calling out a target, and doing it for fun or to make some kind of statement, as opposed to attacking for financial gain."[18] But experts also acknowledge that even hacking done for fun can cause damage to individuals, businesses, and/or governments.

Facts

- On June 1, 1990, phreaker Kevin Poulsen seized control of a radio station's phone lines so that he could ensure he would be the 102nd caller in a contest that awarded that caller with a Porsche 944 S2 automobile valued at $50,000.

- Among hackers, a hacker who destroys things—by creating viruses, for example, or bypassing passwords to break into a computer or to violate a website for malicious reasons—is commonly called a cracker.

- The first computer virus was invented in 1983 by a student at the University of Southern California, Fred Cohen, as part of a class experiment, but the virus was never shared outside the computer lab.

- The first hacker magazine, *2600*, was published in 1984 to provide hackers with tips and advice; its name comes from the frequency of the tone used by the first phreakers to access phone lines.

- The first person in Australia to be arrested and convicted for hacking was Nahshon Even-Chaim in April 1990, as a result of his using a dial-up computer to break into the computer networks of defense and nuclear agencies.

What Damage Can Hacking Do to Individuals?

I n the latter half of 2012, a hacking group calling itself Team GhostShell broke into the computer systems of various government agencies and private corporations as part of what the group said was a hacktivist mission. On its Twitter page, Team GhostShell states: "Hacktivists of the 21st century. Taking on governments and private corporations is our way of protest. We are all ghosts living inside the shell."[19]

However, many of their activities exposed individuals to potential harm. For example, in August 2012 the group made public, or leaked, information from 1 million personal accounts acquired by hacking more than 100 companies, and in October it leaked information from 120,000 student and employee records from 100 universities around the world. In December 2012 it leaked about 1.6 million account details from nearly 40 websites. The personal information shared via online postings included user names, e-mail addresses, passwords, phone numbers, bank account numbers, and employee payroll information.

After the university hack, Team GhostShell justified its actions by saying that it was trying to make people cast a critical eye on modern educational systems. In a message posted on an online bulletin board, it said, "We have set out to raise awareness towards the changes made in today's education, how new laws imposed by politicians affect us, our economy and over all, our way of life.

Tuition fees have spiked up so much that by the time you finish any sort of degree, you will be in more debt than you can handle and with no certainty that you will get a job."[20]

GhostShell also seemed to suggest that educational institutions were turning people into little more than data. In its statement it complained, "How far we have ventured from learning valuable skills that would normally help us be prepared in life, to just simply memorizing large chunks of text in exchange for good grades. How our very own traditions are heard less and less, losing touch with who we truly are. Slowly casting the identities, that our ancestors fought to protect, into exile."[21]

Identity Theft

In the wake of the Team GhostShell hacks, a representative at Stanford University, one of the hacked colleges, said, "No restricted or prohibited data was compromised, nor was any sensitive or other personal information that could lead to identity theft."[22] But at other universities the situation was not as positive. Security experts concluded that while some of the stolen information was wrong or out of date, there was enough valid information provided on some of the victims to allow criminals to use it to commit identity theft.

Identity theft is the illegal use of someone else's identity, typically for personal and/or financial gain. The most common reasons behind such thefts are to steal money from bank accounts and to get services without paying for them. An example of the latter is medical identity theft. In this case a person without health insurance uses stolen identification numbers, such as a Social Security number or medical ID number, in order to pretend to be someone else who does have health insurance that will pay for the thief's medical treatments. Knowing someone's Social Security number also allows someone to commit tax identity theft, whereby the thief can steal the victim's tax refund money.

However, computer security experts say that identity theft in-

"Much of the data stolen through computer hacking . . . will end up on a network of illegal trading sites where hackers and criminals from around the world will openly buy and sell large amounts of personal data for profit."[23]

— Privacy Matters, a company devoted to helping people safeguard their credit card numbers.

creasingly involves crime organizations as opposed to individual hackers. Privacy Matters, a company devoted to helping people safeguard their credit card numbers, says:

> Much of the data stolen through computer hacking—including stolen credit card numbers and Social Security numbers—will end up on a network of illegal trading sites where hackers and criminals from around the world will openly buy and sell large amounts of personal data for profit. Stolen data networks have flourished in the open,

Identity theft can take many forms. Some hackers have obtained medical services using stolen medical insurance account numbers or social security numbers.

with names like Network Terrorism Forum, Shadowcrew, Carderplanet, Dark Profits, and Mazafaka.[23]

Privacy Matters reports that one of these networks, Shadowcrew, traded roughly 1.5 million stolen credit card numbers during less than two years of operation, for a profit of more than $5 million.

Password Thefts

According to a study released in February 2013 by fraud researcher Javelin Strategy & Research, credit card numbers are the most common data sought by hackers. However, 16 percent of hacking incidents target Social Security numbers, and 10 percent of incidents involved the theft of user names and passwords. Many of these password thefts involve sites where financial transactions take place, but social networking sites are sometimes hacked for passwords as well.

For example, in June 2012 the password databases of two networking websites, LinkedIn and eHarmony (the former related to business dealings, the latter to dating), were hacked, apparently by the same person. Approximately 6.5 million passwords were stolen from LinkedIn and 1.5 million from eHarmony. In both cases the passwords were hashed, or encrypted, using a hash algorithm that security experts put into place to convert a password into a unique set of numbers and letters. But the hacker posted the hashed passwords on an online forum and asked other hackers to help him crack these codes, and within a short time all but about ninety-eight thousand of the passwords had been cracked.

"In the space of one hour, my entire digital life was destroyed."[25]

— Writer Mat Honan, victim of a serious cyberattack.

There are two main reasons a hacker would go to so much trouble to gain access to social networking passwords. First, many people use the same password, or only slight variations on a basic password, for all of their accounts, which means learning social networking site passwords could lead to knowing banking site passwords. Second, many people engage in daisy-chaining, which means that they link a series of e-mail accounts and devices together.

The Danger of Old Computers

Disposing of an old computer can lead to identity theft if its data has not first been permanently erased. Cyber-security experts say that many computer users either fail to erase the data or do so in an ineffective way, not understanding that wiping the computer clean is not the same as deleting files. Richard Clayton, from Cambridge University's computer laboratory, says, "If you're going to sell your computer you should use a secure way of deleting. There are special programmes which write zeros all over the data which is like putting a big black marker pen over pages." If this is not done the data could fall into the wrong hands—if not those of identity thieves then those of blackmailers who buy old computers specifically to mine them for information and photos that victims will pay to keep private. Clayton says, "Even though you think you have deleted all the files, they are still all there. If you sell your computer on Ebay, another person can use the specialist software to read the information, even though it is like rejigging a puzzle."

Quoted in Urmee Khan, "Old Computers Could Easily Fall Victim to Identity Theft—Even If They Delete Files," *Telegraph* (London), January 7, 2009. www.telegraph.co.uk.

Reporter Memphis Barker did both of these things, until a data breach at the Twitter social networking site made her reconsider her own lax security measures. She says:

Until the beginning of this month [March 2013], I used one tinpot password for pretty much all my activity online. Eight characters long—without numbers or symbols—its prime value was sentimental, the product of a relationship that started in the era of the floppy disk. Then paranoia struck. On 1 February, 250,000 Twitter passwords were stolen by hackers. Had the hackers cracked mine—and found their way to the Gmail and bank account daisy-chained to it—well, they wouldn't quite have been able to retire [on the money they could access], but the fear . . . was enough to spook me into a radical overhaul of my online security.[24]

Writer Mat Honan, however, did not have an opportunity to rethink his online security before he was attacked by a hacker. As a result of this attack, he says,

in the space of one hour, my entire digital life was destroyed. First my Google account was taken over, then deleted. Next my Twitter account was compromised, and used as a platform to broadcast racist and homophobic messages. And worst of all, my AppleID account was broken into, and my hackers used it to remotely erase all of the data on my iPhone, iPad, and MacBook. In many ways, this was all my fault. My accounts were daisy-chained together.[25]

Consequently, Honan lost many documents, e-mails, and irreplaceable family photos that had been stored in his MacBook and nowhere else.

Unsecure Connections

Hackers know that passwords used to access web accounts are vulnerable to their actions, but there are other ways that hackers can steal people's passwords. One of these ways becomes available when a computer user is connected to the Internet via an unsecured wireless, or wi-fi, connection. In such cases when the user visits a website and types in a password, others can get this information. Consequently, hacker Jeremy Schoemaker says that using an unsecured connection is equivalent to a situation where "someone got on the loudspeaker at the Denver International Airport and started yelling out over and over again, 'my Facebook username is Johnny@gmail.com and my password is jerky123.'" Therefore, he says, "If you are using a public network of any kind, wifi or not, expect many people see everything you are doing."[26]

"If you are using a public network of any kind, wifi or not, expect many people see everything you are doing."[26]

— Hacker Jeremy Schoemaker.

This is what happened to a blogger named Ramsey while using an unsecured connection during a vacation in India. He reports, "I was in Delhi sending some emails in a horrid little joint in the main Bazaar. I think that is where it happened but I didn't find out til a week later when I was up in the Himalayas. I tried to log into Facebook and it gave me a warning that my account had been accessed from Bangalore—a hackers mecca and a location I was nowhere near." As soon as he got the warning, Ramsey says, "I checked my email account (not my main one) and found that it had been sending mass emails to my contacts advertising some spam rubbish. Several of the contacts had emailed me to find out what was going on."[27]

Although he is still not sure exactly how his problem started, Ramsey now says, "I think someone had got into my Facebook account and then the email linked to that Facebook account. Luckily for me they hadn't changed the passwords so I was able to get back in and fix the problem."[28] Nonetheless, he experienced some embarrassment in dealing with the people who received the spam. He was also mad at himself for not knowing better than to use an unsecure connection, because he considers himself an experienced Internet user.

But Ramsey recognizes that the damage could have been much worse. He says, "When your Facebook, blog, email or bank accounts get hacked your life can be ruined. Some of us spend our entire existences online and such a breach can have terrible effects. You can have money stolen, personal details hijacked and, as happened to me, spam emails sent out to hundreds of high profile clients."[29]

"Some of us spend our entire existences online and such a breach can have terrible effects."[29]

— Ramsey, a blogger whose computer accounts were hacked.

Phishing

Spam is a common result of a hack. In fact, computer expert Andy Trask says, "The primary symptom of a hacked email account is that your account suddenly starts sending spam emails to your friends as well as to strangers."[30] Trask reports that the most common causes of this type of hack are phishing e-mails, viruses, Trojan horses, and keystroke loggers (which record whatever is being typed on the computer's keyboard).

A phishing e-mail is a message made to look as though it was sent by a legitimate company. The aim of such an e-mail is to entice recipients to click on a link within the message that in many cases takes the recipient to an equally legitimate-looking but fraudulent website. On this site, users might be tricked into providing personal information such as a credit card number or bank account credentials, sometimes with disastrous results. For example, while living abroad, a woman from England lost $1.6 million in savings after responding to a phishing e-mail sent by a gang of fourteen cybercriminals. The e-mail was made to look like it came from the woman's bank, and when she clicked on the link within the e-mail, it took her to a fake banking website set up by the gang. Once she input her log-in information there, the criminals were able to use it to siphon money from her bank account.

After the criminals were arrested, Detective Inspector Stewart Garrick of a London police unit specializing in electronic crimes said, "This is an example of how cybercrime creates real victims through the indiscriminate actions of the criminals involved. The victim in this case has suffered significant stress after her life savings—which she intended to use to purchase a property on her return to England—were stolen."[31]

Malware

Responding to a phishing e-mail can also expose victims to malware—short for malicious or malevolent software—which can allow a hacker to disrupt and/or gain access to the victim's computer system. There are several kinds of malware. Among the most common are computer viruses and Trojan horses. The viruses used in concert with phishing often involve duping people in much the same way the phishing e-mail does, by tricking individuals into providing the hacker with money in a seemingly voluntary way. For example, one virus infects the computer so that a message pops up to warn that the user's security software is expiring and a renewal fee is due in order to prevent a computer crash. When a computer user pays this fee, the scammer is the one actually receiving the payment.

"The primary symptom of a hacked email account is that your account suddenly starts sending spam emails to your friends as well as to strangers."[30]

— Computer expert Andy Trask.

Many businesses provide Wi-Fi connections for their customers. Computer users who connect to the Internet via an unsecured wireless, or Wi-Fi, location put their computers and their personal information at risk.

Trojan horses also rely on trickery. Often the computer user is duped into intentionally downloading something that seems harmless or opening an e-mail attachment, such as a greeting card, that seems perfectly legitimate. But in actuality, the act of downloading or opening the attachment has secretly brought hidden, malicious software into the computer. (The name *Trojan horse* comes from the story of ancient Greek soldiers who hid inside a wooden horse in order to get into the city of Troy and destroy it.)

Unlike a virus, a Trojan horse is not self-replicating. That is, it does not spread from computer to computer, but instead remains within the computer that has been afflicted by the Trojan horse software. It then provides the hacker with remote access to the computer, making it possible for the hacker to perform such actions as downloading or uploading files to or from the computer, taking complete control of the computer, or crashing the computer so that it can no longer operate.

Often a Trojan horse is designed to allow the hacker to perform actions secretly, without the computer user having any idea of what is happening. In such cases the Trojan horse is considered a type of spyware, which is any software that installs itself on a computer in order to covertly gather information. Such software can allow the hacker to steal data, view things through the computer's webcam (a camera that can transmit images over the Internet), see whatever is being displayed on the computer's screen, or engage in keystroke logging.

Cyberstalking

Cyberstalking and other forms of online harassment can be accomplished without hacking. However, hacking is increasingly a part of these activities. Often such cases involve accessing a social networking site, e-mail account, or computer in order to acquire photographs or send e-mails intended to embarrass the victim. In December 2011, for example, twenty-four-year-old Joseph Bernard Campbell of Largo, Florida, was sentenced to thirty months in prison on federal charges of cyberstalking and unauthorized access to a computer (the legal term for hacking). He was sentenced after he admitted to hacking into the e-mail accounts of approximately five hundred women, some of whom he knew from high school. He did this in order to see whether the women had e-mailed naked or seminaked photographs of themselves to boyfriends. When he found such photographs, he stole them and hacked into the women's Facebook accounts to post the images.

Campbell told authorities that he was able to hack into these women's accounts because they responded to an e-mail saying that someone had sent them an electronic greeting card. To get the card, the recipient was told, it would be necessary for her to key in her e-mail address and password, which the hacker was able to grab without even providing a greeting card. One of the victims later told a reporter that the crime had "mortified" her and made her feel violated. "It wasn't rape or murder," she said, "but it was certainly rape of emotions for the women involved."[32]

Blackmail

Because of the damage the appearance of such photos can cause, some hackers have stolen them from computers for the purpose of blackmail. For example, in November 2011 thirty-two-year-old paraplegic Luis Mijangos, a Mexican citizen living in Southern California, was sentenced to six years in prison for computer hacking and wiretapping. Prosecutors had tied Mijangos to the blackmail of about 230 people, 44 of them minors. His victims were typically users of a peer-to-peer (P2P) network, a type of communication network that lets people share files with other users.

When people on the P2P network downloaded a popular song or video shared there by Mijangos, they also received hidden malware that allowed him to access and control their computers. If they then shared the song or video with others, those people received the hidden malware too. Ultimately, this provided Mijangos with remote access to more than one hundred computers, and because his victims were unaware that their computer security had been violated, he was able to watch them secretly through their own webcams and search their computers covertly for photos showing them nude or seminude.

Once he found such photos, Mijangos sent threats to his victims, telling them that he would share the photos with others unless they sent him pornographic photos and/or videos of themselves. When one woman did not heed this warning, he went through with his threat, posting nude photos of her on a friend's MySpace page. He then continued to blackmail her, saying that if she did not cooperate, he would send more photos to her employer. This victim later told police that whenever she signed on to the computer she used at work, she saw messages reminding her of the consequences of refusing to do what he wanted. Consequently, at

Stolen Tax Refunds

Between 2008 and 2012 cases of identity theft related to income tax returns increased by 650 percent, according to the Internal Revenue Service. A 2012 audit by the US Department of the Treasury revealed that during the previous year, identity thieves used stolen personal information to file 1.5 million fraudulent returns that brought them $5.2 billion in tax refunds. Some of these criminals have the money refunded to an address that cannot be tied to them, such as a vacant house with an unmonitored mailbox. Others have the refunds sent electronically to a temporary bank account, which lowers their risk of getting caught still further.

In either case, the IRS can take months or years to detect and rectify the problem, which means that criminals are often able to strike a victim more than once. For example, one such victim of ID theft and fraudulent tax returns, 57-year-old Marcy Hossli of Lake Worth, Florida, still had not received her 2010, 2011, or 2012 refunds as of April 2013. "I should never have to go through anything like this, nor should anyone else," she says. "I feel violated. It's hard to concentrate in work. I am stressed constantly."

Quoted in Lindsay Wise, "Tax Refunds Lost to Identity Thieves," *U-T San Diego*, April 12, 2013. www.utsandiego.com.

Mijangos's sentencing hearing, she said, "He haunts me every time I use the computer. You don't have to be in jail to feel trapped."[33]

Too Trusting

Mijangos succeeded in taking control of his victims' computers because they were too trusting. It never occurred to them that a person sharing a seemingly harmless song or video could have a malicious intent. This is a common trait of individuals who become victims of hacking, and hackers continue to come up with new ways to exploit it.

In early 2013, for example, the Federal Trade Commission began warning the public about a new kind of computer scam designed to take advantage of trusting, gullible people. Specifically, a criminal calls someone on the telephone claiming to be working for a major computer company like Microsoft. The criminal then tells the victim that a virus has been detected on that person's computer but adds that the virus can be repaired if the computer user sits at the keyboard and does certain things. Following the caller's instructions often results in the criminal gaining remote access to the computer and/or tricking the computer user into installing malware on the computer or divulging password or credit card information.

Hackers use the term *social engineering* to describe techniques that trick people into letting down their guard. Often this involves researching an intended victim to determine what category of person he or she falls into—such as someone who enjoys downloading songs, for example. Computer security expert Tomer Teller explains:

> While hacking a system requires knowledge of programming vulnerabilities, hacking the human mind requires a different kind of knowledge—specifically, what types of e-mails or links is the victim most likely to click on. One way to get a hold of that information is to target people according to their jobs and interests—and there is perhaps no greater source of data on those subjects than social networks.[34]

Teller reports that by reading profiles on sites like LinkedIn and Facebook, hackers can often find out enough about a person's interests to figure out what special offers, messages, or attachments will interest them. Consequently, computer security experts emphasize that computer users should use strong privacy controls on social networking sites and ignore temptations to open unsolicited attachments or click on links or download files provided by unfamiliar individuals.

Facts

- According to complaints made to the Federal Trade Commission, medical identity theft accounts for approximately 2 percent of cases of identity theft.

- In mid-2012 the credit safeguarding company Privacy Matters reported that hacking had compromised the personal records of approximately 43 million Americans over the previous twelve months.

- Computer security experts report that there are almost four thousand websites on the Internet that tell people how to hack personal and business computers.

- According to a study released by Javelin Strategy & Research in February 2013, over the previous twelve months one in four people who were notified by a company that their personal records had been compromised by a computer security breach ultimately became a victim of identity theft.

- According to the technology blog *Royal Pingdom*, 68 percent of all e-mail traffic worldwide is spam, and 22 percent of e-mails are associated with phishing.

How Does Hacking Harm Businesses?

I n February 2013 a computer security company called Mandiant Corporation issued a report on the theft of intellectual property from the computers of thousands of US businesses. Intellectual property is something created with the mind, such as inventions, sketches, business plans, architectural or industrial designs, trademarks, manuscripts, photographs, and illustrations. The company's clients were businesses wanting to know whether they had been hacked and, if so, by whom. Over a period of seven years, Mandiant had observed that one group was responsible for a large number of these attacks. Operating out of an office building just outside of Shanghai, China, this group stole proprietary information from more than one hundred Mandiant clients associated with twenty industries, including chemical plants, military contracting companies, mining companies, and telecommunications companies. The computer systems of at least 115 companies located in the United States were attacked.

After spying on the group's activities and communications, Mandiant concluded that the hackers' operation was being run by the Chinese army and provided details supporting this conclusion in its report. Company founder Kevin Mandia, a retired military cybercrime investigator, says that he decided to share this conclusion with the public—even though it might cause diplomatic problems between the United States and China—because he wanted the hackers to be held accountable for their actions, which have damaged the US economy. He states, "We probably kicked the hornet's nest" by going public with the information, but "tolerance is just dwindling. People are tired of the status quo of being hacked with impunity, where there's no risk or repercussion."[35]

Other computer security experts lauded Mandiant for going public with this information, and some of them said it was not surprising that the Chinese government would be connected to the hacking. For example, James Lewis, a senior fellow who studies cybersecurity at the Center for Strategic and International Studies in Washington, DC, says, "This has been a part of their plan to catch up to the West. You steal their technology, you steal their business secrets."[36]

However, the release of the report caused Mandiant some trouble. Mandia claims that within hours after it was made public, the hackers sent his employees phishing e-mails in an unsuccessful attempt to gain control of the company's computer systems. The hackers also created a version of Mandiant's report that would infect with a virus any computer that downloaded it, then e-mailed it to various people in the hopes of ruining Mandiant's reputation.

Meanwhile, Mandia says, Chinese officials took various measures in an attempt to hide their involvement in the hacks. For example, they took many of their computers offline and altered information on websites that had been tied to them in Mandiant's report. Shortly after these actions were taken, the Chinese government officially denied being involved in the hacks.

Lost Technology

Shortly after the report's release, the White House issued its own report on the cybertheft of intellectual property, titled "Administration Strategy on Mitigating the Theft of U.S. Trade Secrets." The report agrees that many hacks targeting US businesses originate in China but does not go so far as to say the Chinese army was involved, stating, "Chinese actors are the world's most active and persistent perpetrators of economic espionage. U.S. private sector firms and cybersecurity specialists have reported an onslaught of comput-

> "People are tired of the status quo of being hacked with impunity, where there's no risk or repercussion."[35]
>
> — Kevin Mandia, an expert in cybercrime and cybersecurity.

er network intrusions that have originated in China, but the IC [US Intelligence Community] cannot confirm who was responsible."[37]

For some US businesses, the impact of Chinese hacking has been devastating. One US metallurgical company, for example, suffered the loss of technology that had been in development for twenty years at a cost of $1 billion. Other hard-hit companies have been involved in biotechnology, nanotechnology, or clean energy. Because of such cases General Keith Alexander, director of the National Security Agency, says China's theft of intellectual property constitutes "the greatest transfer of wealth in history."[38] Michael Wessel, part of a commission on US-China economic and security issues that reports to Congress, says, "We need to take more actions and protect our intellectual property."[39]

Vulnerable to Attacks

Technology experts say that it is particularly difficult to fight such thefts because so much information is vulnerable to attack. As technology reporters Michael Riley and Ashlee Vance explain, "China's been helped by good timing. It's emerging as a global economic power at a time when nearly every secret worth stealing sits on a computer server."[40]

Officials say that US businesses are being threatened by hackers in other parts of the world as well. The White House report on the theft of trade secrets specifically cites Russia as being almost as aggressive as China in this regard. It also warns that US allies with seemingly good relationships with US businesses should not be allowed access to sensitive information without careful thought. The intelligence report also forecasts that such threats will continue to grow, both because the United States will continue to have intellectual property worth stealing and because businesspeople are increasingly connecting to the Internet via portable electronic devices that provide more openings for hackers.

"We need to take more actions and protect our intellectual property."[39]

— Michael Wessel, an expert on economic and security issues.

Inside Information

But intellectual property is not the only thing that hackers seek to steal from companies. Sometimes they are looking for inside infor-

The Coca-Cola Corporation was negotiating the purchase of a Chinese company, Huiyuan Juice Group, in 2009 when a hacker attacked Coke's computer systems. Investigators believe the hackers wanted information on the company's negotiating strategy.

mation on a business deal. Such information can enable hackers to profit by making certain investments before the deal is made public, or it can enable them to influence negotiations. The latter was the case when Chinese hackers secretly attacked the computer systems of the Coca-Cola Company in 2009.

At that time, Coca-Cola had offered to acquire a Chinese juice company, the China Huiyan Juice Group, for approximately $2.4 billion. Shortly after this offer was made, the hackers sent a seemingly innocuous e-mail to one of the Coca-Cola executives involved in the deal. When he clicked on the link in the e-mail, he unknowingly brought malware into the company's computer systems. This allowed the hackers complete remote access to the computers.

Over the next two days, the hackers uploaded tools into the computer systems that allowed them to steal e-mails, documents, and employee passwords and to monitor keystrokes. Some of the passwords belonged to top administrators of the computer network, which made it even easier for the hackers to get the information they wanted. Investigators into the security breach later determined that the hackers were primarily interested in learning Coca-Cola's negotiating strategy for the acquisition (which eventually did not come to pass). For at least the next month, the hackers rummaged through the computer systems daily to look for ways to put Coca-Cola at a disadvantage during negotiations, and during this period Coca-Cola was unaware of the breach.

Damaging Attacks

Once Coca-Cola learned what had happened, it did not want anyone outside the company to know that it had been hacked. This is common with major companies that have had security breaches. Information-security expert Michael Oberlaender reports, "They fear that bringing this to the public will do them more harm than good."[41] Corporate executives generally believe that if people knew how vulnerable their computers were at the time of a breach, it would hurt their reputation and damage their relationship with investors.

Sometimes, however, it is impossible for a company to conceal an attack on its computer systems. This is particularly true when the company is an online business whose customers' account information has been stolen. Then the company has an obligation to inform customers that their personal security has been jeopardized—and often when this happens, the media learns of the security breach and reports on it. For example, in January 2012 online shoe and clothing retailer Zappos was hacked and 24 million customer accounts were compromised. The company notified these customers by e-mail that their names, e-mail addresses, phone numbers, passwords, and last four digits of their credit card numbers might have been stolen. They also warned customers that the hackers might send them phishing e-mails in an attempt to get more financial information from them. However, the company insisted that the database where full credit card numbers and other payment information were stored remained secure. It also told customers that when the breach was discovered, the company reset all customer passwords to prevent the hackers from having further access to the accounts.

Secrecy

When this news became public, the media began questioning whether Zappos had acted quickly enough after the breach to notify customers. Meanwhile the company would not say when the breach occurred. It refused to answer other media questions as well, such as whether it knew the full extent of the damage caused by the hack and whether it shared computer systems with Amazon, the company that owns it.

Still, some business reporters noted that Zappos went further than most companies do to address the situation. Nicole Perlroth of the *New York Times* says, "A majority of companies that have at one time or another been the subject of news reports of on-

Millions of customer accounts were compromised by a 2012 hacking attack against the online retailer Zappos (pictured). The company notified customers by e-mail, alerting them to the problem and informing them of steps being taken to prevent further access by the hackers.

line attacks refuse to confirm them."[42] Payment processing company Heartland Payment Systems reported a major data breach in 2009—one of the first companies to do so. The company was advised by its lawyers not to make the breach public, even though millions of its credit and debit card customers had been exposed to fraud. Lawyers are typically concerned that by taking responsibility for notifying clients or customers, a company would also be accepting responsibility for any financial damages caused by the breach.

In 2011 Sony Corporation chose not to notify its customers after their personal information was compromised due to a hack into the company's PlayStation network. Instead it posted the information on a blog, which later led Mary Bono Mack, a member of a US House Energy and Commerce subcommittee addressing the issue of cyberattacks, to complain, "Sony put the burden on consumers to search for information, instead of accepting the burden of notifying them. If I have anything to do with it, that kind of half-hearted, half-baked response is not going to fly in the future."[43]

Similarly, Global Payments, a major payment processor, was criticized in 2012 for concealing the fact that it had experienced two major security breaches exposing millions of accounts to theft. These came to light only because a popular security blogger uncovered the breaches. The company was also criticized for not sharing details about the hack that might have helped other companies protect their computer systems from a similar attack.

Computer security experts say it is critical for companies to work together to try to thwart hackers. To this end, in February 2013 US president Barack Obama signed an executive order urging private companies and government agencies to share more information about online security threats. However, the order does not require private companies to do this, because business lobbyists had fought such a move. Steve Elefant, chief information officer with Heartland, doubts that companies will be any less reluctant to report cyberattacks in the future. "I wouldn't hold my breath," he says. "There are an awful lot of lawyers out there trying

"There are an awful lot of lawyers out there trying to keep companies from exposing that these breaches are happening. And they are happening."[44]

— Steve Elefant, a computer security expert.

to keep companies from exposing that these breaches are happening. And they are happening."[44]

Denial of Service

But hackers can do more than just steal data stored on company computers. They can also shut down a company's website so that it can no longer do business online. Such an attack—or any kind of attack that tries to keep legitimate computer users from accessing information or services via the Internet—is called a denial-of-service (DoS) attack.

There are several types of DoS attacks, targeting either an individual's computer and network connection to the Internet or the computers and network connections of the websites the user is trying to access. In either case the attack can result in a computer user be-

Packet Sniffing

A packet sniffer is a tool used to diagnose problems with a computer network, but it can also be used by hackers to steal information. Packet sniffers intercept inbound and outbound packets of data sent via the Internet and then put the data into a form that the user can understand. This makes it possible to determine what the information is and how efficiently it is moving from one place to another. To this end, the user typically sets up the packet sniffer on a computer so that it will intercept only packets intended for that computer. However, packet sniffers can also be set up to intercept every packet on a network, no matter where it is going, a set-up that is called the promiscuous mode. This is how hackers distort the purpose of the sniffer. They put their own packet sniffer on a network in the promiscuous mode, then use it to intercept all packets so they can view all network traffic, including transmitted passwords.

ing unable to visit websites and/or retrieve e-mail messages. This can cause not only inconvenience but also lost business opportunities.

The most basic type of DoS attack is a coordinated effort that does not involve hacking. Instead, the attacker simply overwhelms a website with so many requests to view it (such "requests" occur every time a person types the site address into the computer's website browser) that the site cannot handle all the Internet traffic and becomes inaccessible. Similarly, a flood of spam e-mails can overwhelm an e-mail account to the point where it can no longer receive new, nonspam e-mails.

In many cases, however, the attacker takes over many other computers in order to accomplish the flooding, typically by hacking strangers' computers using a Trojan horse. Collections of computers that have been put under the control of a hacker's malware in this way are called botnets, and their resulting multisystem attack against a single system is known as a distributed denial-of-service (DDoS) attack because the responsibility for the attack is distributed among several computers. DDoS attacks allow the hacker to flood the target with extremely large volumes of data from perhaps hundreds of thousands of different sources.

A Feared Threat

Given this amount of computer power, botnets can do considerable damage. In his book *Inside Cyber Warfare: Mapping the Cyber Underworld,* Jeffrey Carr reports, "One botnet of one million hosts could conservatively generate enough traffic to take most Fortune 500 companies collectively offline. A botnet of 10 million hosts . . . could paralyze the network infrastructure of a major Western nation."[45]

Consequently, according to computer security expert Aaron Weiss, "Denial of Service (DoS) attacks are among the most feared threats in today's cybersecurity landscape. Difficult to defend against and potentially costly, DoS attacks can cause outages of web sites and network services for organizations large and small." In addition, he says, "DoS attacks effectively knock the services offline, costing lost business and negative publicity. They also force IT [information technology] staff to expend valuable resources defending against the attackers."[46]

In discussing the costs of a DoS attack, Richard Power of the Computer Security Institute says, "If you're conducting e-business and you're counting on $600,000 an hour in revenue, like Amazon, and your service is disrupted by a denial of service attack, you can start with the figure $600,000 for every hour that you're down. If you're Cisco and you're making $7 million a day online, and you're down for a day, you've lost $7 million."[47]

Extortion

Weiss says that criminals often use the fact that DoS attacks are so costly to their advantage. He reports, "The perpetrators choose their victim deliberately, either due to a grudge, revenge, or an attempt to bully them into meeting some demands—possibly including paying extortion" which he says can run into millions of dollars. Moreover, "[t]here is big money in creating botnets—among other things, botnet creators rent out their creations to criminal enterprises who can use them to launch a DDoS. Renting a botnot to launch a DDoS can cost about $100 per day, so the duration of an attack is partially dependent on how well-funded the attacker [is]."[48]

In most cases both forms of denial-of-service attacks are a way to get money from the target or to punish the target as a result of various grievances. The latter was the case, for example, with DDoS attacks in 2010 against the credit card companies Visa and MasterCard and the money-transferring company PayPal by the hacker group Anonymous. Members of the group posted an explanation of their actions online, describing the attacks (which they called "Operation Payback") as punishment for a decision by the three companies to no longer aid WikiLeaks, an online organization that published leaked documents, in collecting donations online for its activities.

In commenting on the effects of the Anonymous attacks, computer security expert Noa Bar Yossef says:

> Operation Payback's goal is not hacking for profit. In the classical external hacker case we see hackers grab information from wherever they can and monetize on it. In this

case though, the hackers' goal is to cripple a service, disrupt services, protest their cause and cause humiliation. In fact, what we see here is a very focused attack—knocking the servers offline due to so-called "hacker injustice."[49]

In some cases, however, a DoS or DDoS attack is a distraction for other, less principled activities. In 2011, for example, Anonymous launched an attack against Sony Corporation ostensibly as punishment for the company taking hacker George Hotz to court. (Hotz had found a way to get the company's PlayStation gaming system to play games other than Sony's, including pirated games, and then shared information about his hack online.) While the company was dealing with the Anonymous attack, however,

Computer Specialists

Corporations typically rely on computer security specialists, also called information security specialists, to protect their computer systems from threats coming from both inside and outside the company. These computer experts, who typically have at least a bachelor's degree in computer science or technology, have several duties. Among these is the control of passwords within the company, which involves not only restricting who can know passwords but also making sure passwords are changed regularly. Other duties include installing and regularly updating software to protect the system and dealing with the aftermath of a security breach should it occur. Computer security specialists are expected to back up all information on a regular basis so that if a breach wipes out data in one place it can be restored from another. In addition, computer security specialists are often required to keep informed about new advances in computer technology and new threats to computer systems.

A denial of service attack can have particularly damaging effects on online retailers such as Amazon, whose warehouse is pictured here. Financial damages can run into the millions.

someone used the chaos as an opportunity to launch an attack on the PlayStation network, thereby compromising the personal account information of 12.3 million customers. Although Anonymous denies involvement in this attack, Sony believes someone with the group was responsible. Kazuo Hirai, chair of the board of Sony Computer Entertainment America, later called this "a very carefully planned, very professional, highly sophisticated criminal cyber attack."[50]

Disgruntled Employees

Sometimes cyberattacks by organized groups are aided by disgruntled employees. In March 2013, for example, a federal grand jury indicted Matthew Keys, a former employee of the news organization Tribune Company, for giving hackers from Anonymous information that enabled them to access Tribune websites and for conspiring with them to transmit information that would damage a Tribune computer. Keys had reported on the group's hacking activities after moving on to a new job with the Reuters news agency, and he claimed that his suspicious activities were tied to his investigative journalism. However, the US attorney prosecuting the case, Benjamin Wagner, is convinced that Keys's actions were that of someone seeking revenge against a former employer rather than of a journalist chasing a story.

Security experts say that it is not uncommon for laid-off or fired employees to hack into the computers and computer networks at their former jobs. Sometimes they simply use passwords that were not changed after they were let go. Other times they have inside knowledge about the company's computer system that makes hacking relatively easy. Such hacks can cause a lot of damage, especially when the former employee not only disrupts systems but steals money. The computer security company Privacy Matters reports that a thief with insider knowledge and a valid password stole more than $100 million over a two-year period by accessing customer credit card information via the computers of a former employer in New York. Privacy Matters suggests that such criminals rarely feel bad about what they have done, saying, "If employees are disgruntled or angry after they leave the business, maybe because they were fired, they may justify their actions by convincing themselves it's 'just compensation' for money they should have been paid."[51]

In fact, computer security experts say that even current employees could be motivated to commit this kind of theft. Consequently, as the security company Securelist notes, "A company

"A company must secure itself against internal attacks just as effectively as it does against external intrusions."[52]

— Security company Securelist.

must secure itself against internal attacks just as effectively as it does against external intrusions."[52] But with so many possible routes of attack, it is extremely difficult for companies to do this. Therefore, many pay thousands of dollars to specialists in computer security who work year-round to try to safeguard businesses from hacking attacks.

Facts

- Recent surveys indicate that businesses are losing approximately 60 percent more money through cybercrime, particularly hacking, than other types of crime.

- According to security consulting firm Frost & Sullivan, the amount of money spent on data-vulnerability management may grow to almost $1 billion in 2016 from $400 million in 2012.

- According to the Ponemon Institute, in 2011 the total cost of a significant data breach, including all its repercussions, in US dollars was $5.5 million for companies in the United States, $4.4 million for companies in Germany, and $2.7 million for companies in the United Kingdom.

- The Identity Theft Research Center reports that in 2011 nearly 40 percent of recorded data breaches were malicious attacks, which it defined as a combination of hacking and insider theft.

- One of the most destructive computer viruses in history, the Blaster worm, spread over computer networks in 2003 to infect hundreds of thousands of computers running the Microsoft operating system, causing up to $10 billion in damages.

How Does Hacking Affect Countries?

I n January 2013 hackers claiming to be part of the hacktivist group Anonymous posted a "declaration of war" message and a YouTube video on a US government website. They said that several US government computer systems had been secretly hacked as part of an elaborate operation and that their goal in doing this was to force changes in how the country's laws address computer crimes. The hackers' statement read, in part, "Through this website and various others that will remain unnamed, we have been conducting our own infiltration. . . . We have enough fissile material for multiple warheads. Today we are launching the first of these. Operation Last Resort has begun."[53]

The "fissile material" was sensitive information, and the "multiple warheads" referred to nine encrypted files, each named for a different US Supreme Court justice. Links to these files were posted on the government website. The group also posted a warning: If the government did not reform computer crime laws, the hackers would release information that would allow others to decode the files to reveal government secrets.

Serious or Trivial?

The attack was purported to be tied to the January 2013 suicide of 26-year-old Aaron Swartz, a prominent computer programmer, website cofounder, and Internet activist. Swartz was awaiting trial

Members of the hacktivist group Anonymous hold a rally in Boston in 2013 to express their anger over the suicide of Internet activist Aaron Swartz (shown in enlarged photograph). Swartz killed himself while awaiting trial on charges related to documents he obtained from protected computers.

for allegedly obtaining documents from protected computers, an illegal act under the Computer Fraud and Abuse Act. He had downloaded much of a digital library of scholarly articles, then available only through a subscription service, so it could be made available to the public for free. Many hackers considered this action to be either a minor offense or something that should not be illegal at all, yet had Swarz been convicted he could have faced up to 35 years of federal imprisonment and a $1 million fine. To protest this, Operation Last Resort started with an attack on the US Sentencing Commission website (ussc.gov).

The first warhead the hackers released, however, proved to be a dud, according to an Internet newspaper called the *Daily Dot*. After the initial attack, the *Daily Dot* received an e-mail claiming to contain information from one of the hackers' files—the real names of people reassigned new identities as part of the US government's witness protection program. Upon investigation, however, the names proved to be drawn from a list that had already been re-

leased by Anonymous two years earlier, and the e-mail appeared to have been sent from Iran. A few days later the *Daily Dot* reported that a hacker attempting to use decryption information provided by the Operation Last Resort attackers for reading the linked files realized that they were not encrypted after all.

Not Easy to Fix

Because the files released proved harmless, and because the sentencing commission's website is not involved in the day-to-day operation of government, some public officials did not consider the attack to be serious. Even so, as soon as government computer experts learned of the security breach, they took the website offline and began working to repair it. The next day they put it back online, seemingly good as new. On the third day after the attack, however, they realized the website still had a problem.

Hackers had posted instructions at various online sites telling computer users to go to the US Sentencing Commission website and type a series of keystrokes they called the Konami code. Anyone who did this discovered that their keyboard could be used as a video game controller that enabled them to "shoot" the image on the website. When they did this, the image transformed into the symbol of Anonymous, a mask, and then the site became a playable version of the video game *Asteroids*. The hackers subsequently posted information on how another government site, that of the US Probation Office in a district of Michigan, could be made to turn into *Asteroids* too, proving that they had taken over more than just the US Sentencing Commission website.

Unknown Attackers

The attackers' identities, however, could not be confirmed. An Anonymous representative communicating through an Internet account known to be tied to the group insisted that Anonymous had not been behind Operation Last Resort. This person stated, "ALL credible sources/anon cells to date have no idea who is running this operation. It came out of thin air and is using old anon operations data claiming its new."[54]

The Anonymous representative also suggested that the

Hampering Cybercrime Hunters

The Computer Fraud and Abuse Act makes it illegal for private researchers to hack servers (computers that link other computers together) even for the purpose of ridding them of malicious software and/or tracking down the hacker behind the software. Such work, government officials say, is the domain of government security experts. But computer security experts in the private sector counter that this is a foolhardy approach to addressing the problem of hacking. Raimund Genes of the cybersecurity company Trend Micro explains, "They need us, because there are not enough cyber defenders in the government. We have well paid experts who have been around for a quite a while and build a reputation—offering this in a government job is very unlikely." Such experts also point out that because the government has limited resources and more rules to follow in investigating cases, it often moves more slowly than a private company in resolving hacking incidents. For example, after Trend Micro uncovered and reported the existence of a botnet of 4 million computers being used to spread malware, it took the FBI four years to shut down the operation and arrest several members of the Estonian cybercrime ring behind it.

Quoted in Aliya Sternstein, "Anti-Hacking Laws Hamper Private Efforts to Hunt Cybercriminals," *Nextgov Newsletter*, March 27, 2013. www.nextgov.com.

government might be behind the operation—seeing it as a way to encourage tougher hacking laws. But others doubt that the government would hack its own sentencing website or that it would incorporate an *Asteroids* game in the attack. Instead, most people familiar with the attack now suspect it was carried out by old-style hackers showing off their computer prowess while tying it to a cause to justify their actions.

Financial Infrastructure

Though Operation Last Resort caused no real damage, it raised concerns about the government's ability to address a major hacking attack. Another attack, apparently by the same group, heightened those concerns. Less than a week after the attack on the sentencing website, hackers breached the website of the Alabama Criminal Justice Information Center in order to post a spreadsheet there that displayed private information of more than forty-six hundred executives at banks and credit unions. This information appeared to have come from computers at the Federal Reserve Bank, which provides services such as same-day electronic money and funding transfers, that connect it to the entire US banking system.

The Federal Reserve responded to the hack as though it were a nonevent. It stated, "Exposure was fixed shortly after discovery and is no longer an issue. This incident did not affect critical operations of the Federal Reserve system."[55] But security experts suspected the Federal Reserve was minimizing the problems in order to prevent fears about the safety of the nation's financial system.

However, government officials have acknowledged that the nation's financial institutions are at risk of a severe attack, perhaps by domestic or foreign terrorists who want to disrupt the stability of the country. For example, after a 2011 attack that occurred on NASDAQ, a computerized system involved in the trading of the nation's stocks, Gordon M. Snow, then assistant director of the Cyber Division of the FBI, told a Senate judiciary committee on crime and terrorism that "given enough time, motivation, and funding, a determined adversary will likely be able to penetrate any system that is accessible directly from the Internet."[56]

In citing concerns about the nation's financial infrastructure, Snow said, "It is difficult to state with confidence that our critical infrastructure—the backbone of our country's economic prosperity, national security, and public health—will remain unscathed and always be available when needed." In addition, he reported, "The FBI has identified the most significant cyber threats to our nation as those with high intent and high capability to inflict damage or death in the U.S., to illicitly acquire assets, or to illegally obtain sensitive or classified U.S. military, intelligence, or economic information."[57]

Sabotage

Domestic or foreign terrorists might be behind such cyberattacks, but these attacks can also be committed by one nation against another. An example of the latter might have occurred in March 2013. At that time, a company called Telvent, which monitors oil and gas pipelines across the United States, discovered that hackers operating out of China had been trying to plant bugs in its computer systems. The company immediately took steps to prevent this, but it also notified US intelligence agencies of the attempted attack. The company's computer experts suspected that the People's Liberation Army of China might be behind the attacks. If the United States and China ever had a significant conflict, the computer bugs might enable China to cut off energy supplies and shut down the power grid in the United States.

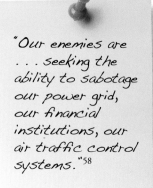

"Our enemies are . . . seeking the ability to sabotage our power grid, our financial institutions, our air traffic control systems."[58]

— US president Barack Obama, in his 2013 State of the Union address.

When this suspicion came to light, China denied having anything to do with the Telvent attack. Nonetheless, in Barack Obama's 2013 State of the Union address, he said, "Our enemies are . . . seeking the ability to sabotage our power grid, our financial institutions, our air traffic control systems."[58] In calling for legislation to protect the nation's infrastructure from cyberattacks, the president warned that such attacks could cause mass casualties.

Serious Repercussions

In fact, a report declassified and released to the public in November 2012 by the National Academy of Sciences states that a terrorist attack on the US power grid would be more destructive than a superstorm, costing perhaps hundreds of billions of dollars and thousands of lives. Most deaths would not happen immediately, the report said, but after weeks or months of dealing with no power. This situation would result in reduced medical care due to a lack of electrically powered medical equipment, exposure to the elements because of the loss of heating and air-conditioning, and shortages of water and natural gas since both are typically supplied via systems that rely on electrically run pumps and compressors.

According to one of the researchers behind the report, senior scientist Alan Crane, the lack of water would be the most serious of these problems. "Living without electricity is one thing," he says. "Living without water is something else."[59] Moreover, the damage done to the power system would not be easy to fix, because cyberterrorists would be able to disable transformers in ways that could take years to fix or replace. There would also be emotional damage to deal with. The report states, "An event of this magnitude and duration could lead to turmoil, widespread public fear, and an image of helplessness that would play directly into the hands of the terrorists."[60]

In response to such reports, and because attempts to use hacking to cause serious damage seem to be increasing, experts have urged the government to take quick action to address the threat of cyberattacks. According to the US Department of Homeland Se-

In his 2013 State of the Union address, President Barack Obama warned the nation that enemies abroad are trying to develop ways to hack into and sabotage the power grid. Such an attack would likely bring all activity to a standstill and significantly threaten health and safety.

curity, 198 cyberattacks on systems deemed critical to the nation's infrastructure were reported to the agency in 2012, a 52 percent increase over the previous year. Among the most worrisome attacks was one in which a hacker gained access to the computer systems of an American defense contractor. Another was an attack against a company that provides Internet security for American spies.

In 2013 one of the most significant cyberattacks involved the hacking of fourteen computer servers and twenty workstations at the Washington, DC, headquarters of the US Department of Energy. Although no classified information was accessed, it was still a serious enough event for (then) Secretary of Defense Leon Panetta to say it was a harbinger of a future "cyber Pearl Harbor"[61] attack on the United States as a whole. In addition, James Arlen, a senior security consultant with the Leviathan Security Group, suggests that spies engaging in computer hacking on behalf of a nation planning to launch a traditional war could gain "advanced knowledge of weaknesses or advanced knowledge of weapons."[62]

Iranian Threat

National security experts disagree, however, on which foreign nation might pose the greatest threat to the security of America's infrastructure. Some cite China as the most threatening, because China engages in so many hacking attacks. However, others argue that China is primarily interested in stealing intellectual property and would not be likely to sabotage America's infrastructure because of China's many investments in the United States. On the other hand, these experts say, Iran has no US investments, which means it would not be hurt economically by an attack on America's infrastructure, and it dislikes America enough to want to sabotage its computer systems. As one unnamed American military official told a reporter with the *New York Times*, "There's nothing but upside for them [the Iranians] to go after American infrastructure."[63]

According to US security experts, Iran might have already launched a cyberattack against US banks. Credit for this attack, which occurred in January 2013, was claimed by a terrorist group, which said the attack was punishment for the appearance in the United States of an anti-Islam video called *The Innocence of Mus-*

lims. But experts believe the attack was too sophisticated to be anything but a state-sponsored effort. It disrupted online banking sites of Wells Fargo, Bank of America, Citigroup, and Capital One, among others. Some sites shut down for several minutes, others were inaccessible for only a few seconds or minutes, while still others merely exhibited a slowing of activity. Carl Herberger, vice president of security firm Radware, which helped investigate the attack, says, "The scale, the scope and the effectiveness of these attacks have been unprecedented. There have never been this many financial institutions under this much duress."[64]

Rather than hacking individual computers or the computer systems of bank branches, the hackers hit computer networks. They did this by first taking control of the computers housed in data centers, which are supposedly secure facilities that provide technology services to businesses unable or unwilling to have their own computer systems. The hackers had infected these computers with malware that allowed them to launch DDoS attacks via the data centers. Technology reporters Nicole Perlroth and Quentin Hardy of the *New York Times* explain, "How, exactly, attackers are hijacking data centers is still a mystery."[65] Experts also say that the DDoS attacks were a new kind, which they labeled an encryption DDoS. It exploited the fact that banks encrypt customers' online transactions for security and flooded banking sites with encryption requests in order to overload them. This caused severe disruptions in service, which was their goal, rather than stealing money.

> "The scale, the scope and the effectiveness of these attacks have been unprecedented."[64]
>
> — Carl Herberger, vice president of the Radware security firm, on foreign attacks on the US banking system.

Denials of Responsibility

Iran was also blamed for an August 2012 cyberattack against the Saudi Arabian oil company Saudi Aramco. In this case thirty thousand computers abruptly stopped functioning in order to display an image of an American flag on fire. One of the company's vice presidents, Abdullah al-Saadan, subsequently told a television reporter, "The main target in this attack was to stop the flow of oil and gas to local and international markets and thank God they were not able to achieve their goals."[66]

Like China, Iran denies that it was behind this attack or any other. But other countries suspected of being behind cyberattacks simply remain silent on the issue. Such is the case with North Korea, which some cybersecurity experts believe has spent years preparing to launch a cyberwar against its enemies. As evidence, they point to an event that took place in July 2009. At that time unknown hackers launched DDoS attacks against twenty-six foreign websites, including that of the White House and other US and South Korean government sites. The attacks appear to have originated from a North Korean university, and many experts think the hackers were associated with the North Korean government.

Tracking down the source of such sophisticated cyberattacks is difficult, but countries around the world are beginning to give significant attention to this issue. This is because national security experts believe cyberwarfare might someday become the weapon of first choice in a war between nations. James Lewis, a cybersecurity expert with the Center for Strategic and International Studies in Washington, DC, says, "There are 12 countries developing offensive cyberweapons. . . . Like nuclear weapons, eventually they'll get there."[67]

In an effort to combat such threats, national security experts in the United Kingdom launched an investigation into that country's vulnerability to cyberattacks. The investigation revealed that the country's armed forces are using technology that might result in the loss of valuable data in the event of a sustained cyberattack. A January 2013 government defense committee report on the matter stated, "The evidence we received leaves us concerned that with the armed forces now so dependent on information and communications technology, should such systems suffer a sustained cyber-attack, their ability to operate could be fatally compromised."[68]

> "The evidence we received leaves us concerned that with the armed forces now so dependent on information and communications technology, should such systems suffer a sustained cyber-attack, their ability to operate could be fatally compromised."[68]
>
> — A January 2013 UK government defense committee report.

The Third Level

According to Kaspersky Lab, an international company that specializes in advanced computer security software, the malware used

by hackers as cyberweapons is different from other types. A 2012 Kaspersky security bulletin on cyberweapons says there are three levels of malware, with the levels best represented by a pyramid. At the bottom, or first, level, the malware has been designed for cybercrime, particularly involving attempts to acquire money. The second, somewhat smaller, level consists of malware that targets organizations in order to steal information or intellectual property from a specific target. The third level—the top level of the pyramid, and the smallest—is made up of malware that experts would consider to be cyberweapons. The report states, "In our classification, this includes malware created and financed by government-controlled structures. Such malware is used against citizens, organizations and agencies in other countries."[69]

Kaspersky Lab states that after examining all known programs of this type, it has identified three main groups of cyberweapons. It calls weapons in the first group destroyers, which are "programs

Iran was blamed for a 2012 cyberattack on the Saudi Arabian oil company, Saudi Aramco (pictured). Company officials believe the goal of the hackers was to halt the flow of oil to international markets.

Cyberwar Threats

Sometimes hacking groups inject themselves into international politics. In April 2013 Anonymous announced Operation Free Korea, whereby it would hack North Korean websites until the country's leader, Kim Jong-un, agreed to resign and the North Korean government agreed to abandon its nuclear program. To show that it was serious, Anonymous released over fifteen thousand passwords taken from a North Korean propaganda website and declared that it would eventually wipe out all of the country's data. It then hacked the country's official Twitter and Flickr accounts as well as four additional North Korean propaganda websites.

While some people support the group's attacks on North Korea, especially in light of the country's threats to launch nuclear attacks on Japan and other US allies, many are worried that this will make North Korea more dangerous. For example, Daniel Perez of the technology website Ubergizmo says, "As much as we appreciate Anonymous' efforts, we have a weird feeling somehow North Korea will take this as a U.S.-based cyber attack, which will result in things only escalating further. At this point, they're looking for any reason at all to do anything to anyone these days."

Daniel Perez, "Anonymous Hacks North Korean Social Networks as Part of 'Operation Free Korea,'" Ubergizmo, April 4, 2013. www.ubergizmo.com.

designed to destroy databases and information as a whole"—that is, to wipe all information from a computer system. Weapons in the second group are espionage programs, whose purpose is "to collect as much information as possible, particularly very highly specialized data . . . which can then be used to create other types of threats." Weapons in the third group are cybersabotage tools.

Of this third group, the report says, "These are the ultimate form of cyber weaponry—threats resulting in physical damage to targets. . . . Threats of this kind are unique and we believe they are always going to be a rare phenomenon. However, some countries are devoting more and more effort to developing this type of threat, as well as defending themselves against it."[70]

A prominent example of such a threat is the Stuxnet worm, which most experts believe was created by the United States and Israel to attack Iran's nuclear facilities. Discovered in June 2010, it is a type of virus called a computer worm—a self-replicating, standalone malware program designed to spread via a computer network—and it was engineered to target only Siemens industrial software and equipment. Iran employs this software and equipment in its nuclear program, and the Stuxnet worm can spy on their use and subvert their activities.

Threatening the Globe

Targeted attacks like the one that involved the Stuxnet worm might not represent the same level of threat as a nuclear weapon. However, security experts warn that cyberattacks between nations can have unintentional consequences—and not just for the country that originates the attack. A cyberattack against the computer system of one nation could conceivably affect the systems of other nations. Cyberweapons expert Pierluigi Paganini states, "One of the most dangerous effects of the use of a cyber weapon is the difficulty to predict its diffusion. Cyber space has no boundaries."[71]

For this reason, many security experts say it is vital for nations to start thinking about coming to some agreement about how the most destructive cyberweapons can and should be used. Otherwise, there might be widespread, perhaps unintentional, damage not only to digital infrastructures but also to the global economy. In February 2013, for example, the UK-based international news magazine the *Economist* called on the United States to engage in serious talks with other nations on how to limit risks related to cyberattacks, saying, "America is not an innocent in the world of cyber-spying. It does plenty itself, and acknowledges that these operations are a legitimate part of national security. At the same time, however, it should do more to promote the idea that everyone would gain from 'cyberarms control' to set the rules of engagement."[72] Otherwise, experts suggest, attacks that threaten national security will not only continue but escalate.

Facts

- In his 2010 book *Cyber War*, US government security expert Richard A. Clarke coined the phrase *cyber warfare* to refer to any actions by one nation to penetrate another nation's computers or networks in order to cause damage or disruption.

- In 2010 the US government created the US Cyber Command (USCYBERCOM) for the dual purpose of defending American military networks from cyberattacks and conducting military cyberspace operations.

- According to Kaspersky Lab, malware created by criminals for the purposes of direct financial gain accounts for more than 90 percent of all current malware threats.

- Researchers in the causes of cyberattacks report that less than 10 percent of such attacks are motivated by cyberespionage or cyberwar, whereas the motivation of the remainder are roughly divided between hactivism and crime.

- A 2011 study by the Electric Power Research Institute found that roughly $3.7 billion in investment is needed to protect the US power grid from cyberattacks.

Can Hacking Be Prevented?

O n March 7, 2012, the US government staged a mock cyber-attack that showed what would probably happen if hackers were to shut down New York City's power grid. The resulting blackouts, train derailments, and other catastrophes would likely cause hundreds of deaths and billions of dollars in damages and financial losses. When members of the US Senate were briefed on these costs, many expressed shock and dismay. However, the exercise did not convince them to pass pending legislation designed to strengthen America's digital infrastructure against attack.

This legislation, the Cybersecurity Act of 2012, would have re-quired private companies involved in activities vital for the nation's infrastructure (such as utility companies and chemical plants) to improve their computer security. However, lobbyists for such companies convinced many members of Congress that it would be too much of an economic hardship for businesspeople to finance these improvements and suggested that the cost was essentially a cybersecurity tax. After the bill failed to pass, the law's supporters acknowledged that financial concerns would likely continue to be an issue with such legislation in the future. Melissa Hathaway, a former White House cyber official under both Barack Obama and George W. Bush, says, "Until someone can argue both the nation-al security and the economic parts of it, you're going to have these dividing forces. Most likely, big industry is going to win because at the end of the day our economy is still in trouble. You can't have an unaffordable tax on industry, not in these times."[73]

There were also disagreements over which government agency

would enforce this and other aspects of the law, and Internet activists complained that regardless of the agency enforcing it, the law would give the government too much power over online activities. In addition, critics of the law said the determination of which companies would have to implement stronger security measures would be too subjective. Reporters Michael Riley and Eric Engleman explain:

> The law would only apply to computer systems whose hacking could result in mass casualties or significant economic damage. Bank of America, yes. Taco Bell, no. Rather than try to regulate entire industries, DHS [the Department of Homeland Security] would identify their most sensitive parts—a certain chemical plant, or a hub in the country's telecommunications network. But how they'd choose was unclear. Should major online retailers fall under the law? Should doctors' offices? The bill didn't say.[74]

Nonetheless, many people knowledgeable about the damage that cyberattacks can do say that having stronger cybersecurity laws, even flawed ones, is vital for national security. In July 2012 US Army general Keith Alexander, director of the National Security Agency, told Congress that the cyberattacks that had occurred so far have been

The US government staged a mock cyberattack in 2012 to demonstrate what would probably happen if hackers succeeded in shutting down the New York City power grid. The city, shown here all lit up at night, would likely experience a whole array of catastrophes were this to occur.

practice runs for greater attacks to come. Others agree and complain that lawmakers are not taking such threats seriously enough. As former executive assistant director of the FBI Shawn Henry says, "Based on my experience, very few people . . . [in Congress] get this. You can't see it, touch it, or taste it, so it's somehow not real."[75]

Protecting Government and Banking Computers

Some existing laws deal with various aspects of cybercrime, such as software piracy. In addition, the Identity Theft and Assumption Deterrence Act and the Economic Espionage Act, which were created to address offline crimes, have been applied to hacker cases even though they were not written for this purpose. But the primary law applied to hacking cases is the Computer Fraud and Abuse Act (CFAA).

The original intent of this law, which was enacted in 1984, was to prevent dangerous hackers from disrupting the nation's banking system or gaining access to classified military information. Consequently, its provisions originally protected only the computers of the federal government and large financial institutions. But thanks to subsequent changes in the law, it can now be applied to every US computer.

The law makes it a federal crime for someone to access a computer without authorization or to exceed the scope of any authorization given. It also makes it a federal crime to transfer, deliver, or communicate information obtained from a computer to someone not authorized to have this information. In addition, it prohibits people from stealing financial information or committing fraud or extortion via a computer, as well as from trafficking in computer passwords or transmitting codes that could interfere with a government computer or with interstate commerce.

A Broad Law

Congress has amended the law seven times at the urging of the US Department of Justice, which wanted to be able to use the law against more types of computer crimes and to punish people convicted of such crimes more harshly. Many major technology and security companies have supported these changes. However, with each amendment the law has become not only broader but vaguer. For example, a 1996 amendment forbids people from accessing "protected computers," but it does not define "protected." Consequently, the courts have determined that this word refers to any computer connected to the Internet and that the law is considered violated even when an unauthorized person using a protected computer does not succeed in accessing any of its data.

Other aspects of the CFAA are also open to interpretation. For example, Tim Wu, a Columbia Law School professor, says, "The Computer Fraud and Abuse Act is the most outrageous criminal law you've never heard of. It bans 'unauthorized access' of computers, but no one really knows what those words mean."[76]

Given such problems, many people have proposed that the law be changed so that it is more specific and defines crimes more narrowly. But when the House Judiciary Committee put forth a new draft of the CFAA in early 2013, it included expansions that did the opposite. Orin Kerr, a professor of law at the George Washington University Law School in Washington, DC, says of the proposed version:

This language is really, really broad. If I read it correctly, the language would make it a felony to lie about your age on an online dating profile if you intended to contact someone online and ask them personal questions. It would make it a felony crime for anyone to violate the TOS [terms of service, or rules of usage] on a government website. . . . In short, this is a step backward, not a step forward. This is a proposal to give DOJ [the Department of Justice] what it wants, not to amend the CFAA in a way that would narrow it.[77]

Fears and Overuse

Critics of the CFAA have suggested that the DOJ's push for broader laws is based on fear. Harvey Silverglate, a criminal defense attorney in Cambridge, Massachusetts, says, "The Department of Justice is kind of phobic in this area. Phobia and panic has really led to, I think, a lot of the overuse and the abusive use of the CFAA."[78] Much of this overuse, critics say, has been directed toward journalists, activists, and security researchers whose computer activities have put the government and/or businesses in a bad light.

As an example, some cite the punishment that gray-hat hacker Andrew Auernheimer received in March 2013. He was sentenced to forty-one months in prison for providing information to a colleague about a weakness that Auernheimer discovered in an AT&T website. Auernheimer told a journalist at the website Gawker about the security breach in order to publicize the problem with the site. By this time the colleague had already downloaded 114,000 e-mail addresses belonging to people who owned Apple iPads. Auernheimer was also ordered to pay $73,000 to AT&T, which suffered negative publicity as a result of the breach.

Deterrence?

Many people have complained about the harsh sentences allowed under the existing CFAA law. However, the new version would mandate even harsher sentences. For example, being convicted of crimes that under the existing law would bring a sentence of up to twenty years in prison would, under the new version of the law, result in up to eighty years. New York University law professor James Grimmelmann calls this potential sentence "simply obscene,"[79] while Robert Holleyman, head of a software trade group, argues, "It is important for laws and law enforcement to be strengthened in appropriate proportions, so that innocent and minor infractions are not over-penalized, but serious crimes are effectively deterred."[80]

Experts disagree, however, on whether tough laws and punishments actually deter hacking. Some studies do suggest that when law enforcement is given more power to arrest and prosecute hackers, the total number of computer attacks goes down. For example, a 2011 investigation by Verizon using data breach cases from

"The Department of Justice is kind of phobic in this area. Phobia and panic has really led to, I think, a lot of the overuse and the abusive use of the CFAA."[78]

— Harvey Silverglate, a criminal defense attorney in Cambridge, Massachusetts.

Verizon, the Secret Service, and the National Hi-Tech Crime Unit (NHTCU) showed a significant reduction in breaches following the 2008 enactment of the Identity Theft Enforcement and Restitution Act, which expanded many aspects of the CFAA. Specifically, from 2008 through 2010 the number of reported breaches fell from 361 million records to 4 million.

However, some cybercrime experts say that such reductions do not mean that hacking is being reduced, simply that fewer hackers are being caught. Marc Rogers, a former law enforcement officer who investigated more than two hundred cybercrime cases over a period of thirteen years, says, "We don't even know how many of these [cybercrime] activities are going on. We're only aware of a fraction of what's happening. That makes it a very hard problem to deal with."[81]

Lack of Resources

Eugene Spafford, a professor of computer science at Purdue University in Lafayette, Indiana, agrees that law enforcement is only able to address a fraction of the hacking cases that need attention. He says, "If you look at the sheer volume—the number of compromises, record disclosures, bank fraud, identity theft—that are occurring weekly in the U.S. alone, these numbers are at least in the tens of thousands of incidents, if not hundreds of thousands. . . . The response has been nowhere near proportional to the need."[82]

One reason so many hacking cases go unaddressed is the fact that crime units often lack the funds and properly trained personnel to investigate cybercrimes. Investigating a hacking case requires a great deal of time and effort as computer experts try to track down the culprit and gather enough evidence to prove that a hacker is guilty. For example, investigators might have to search a hacker's house, confiscate computers, and work to recover data from those computers that might help build a case against the hacker. In addition, since cybercrimes can cross state lines and international boundaries, authorities sometimes have to deal with problems associated with getting records and help from people in distant places.

"It is important for laws and law enforcement to be strengthened in appropriate proportions, so that innocent and minor infractions are not over-penalized, but serious crimes are effectively deterred."[80]

— Robert Holleyman, president and CEO of a software trade group.

Bragging Rights

While some hackers take careful measures to avoid being caught by authorities, others cannot help bragging about their hacking accomplishments, usually to their detriment. This was the case, for example, with twenty-one-year-old Joshua Holly, who engaged in a phishing scheme to steal credit card numbers. He used stolen celebrity photographs, which he acquired via hacking, to lure potential victims to a website where he took their payment data for such things as a service whereby, supposedly, a celebrity would call fans and send them a ringtone. In one instance he hacked the Gmail account of American actress and singer-songwriter Miley Cyrus, and afterward he could not resist boasting about what he had done, not only on website forums frequented by hackers but in interviews with bloggers. This brought him to the attention of federal authorities, and the resulting investigation led to Holly's arrest in 2011. He was caught with approximately two hundred stolen credit card numbers in his possession and appears to have made at least $110,000 from his scheme. Because he was a youthful offender, he was sentenced to only three years' probation for spamming and computer fraud instead of the maximum of ten years in prison.

Private Hands

In cases involving computer systems that are associated with vital elements of the nation's infrastructure, some people have suggested that the way to deal with law enforcement's lack of resources is to put the policing of such systems in the hands of private security experts, particularly since many of the computers belong to private companies. For example, Michael Chertoff, the former secretary of homeland security, says, "Most of the infrastructure is in private hands. The government is not going to be able to manage this like the air traffic control system. We're going to have to enlist a large number of independent actors."[83]

Others have suggested the opposite: that the government take greater control of computers vital to national security and infrastructure. But experts in cyberwarfare say this would cause problems in cases of international cyberattacks because of the complexities of dealing with such attacks. Jeffrey Carr, author of *Inside Cyber Warfare: Mapping the Cyber Underworld*, explains, "International acts of cyber conflict (commonly but inaccurately referred to as cyber warfare) are intricately enmeshed with cyber crime, cyber security, cyber terrorism, and cyber espionage. That web of

A Costly Mistake

The first person convicted under the Computer Fraud and Abuse Act was a student at Cornell University, Robert Morris, who in 1988 created what was perhaps the first computer worm spread over the Internet. His creation was meant as a tool to gauge the Internet's size by seeing how much the worm spread. But he made a mistake in designing the way the worm would replicate itself, and this resulted in it infecting some computers multiple times instead of just once. With each infection the computer typically got slower and slower until it crashed. Approximately six thousand government and university computers linked to the Internet were so affected, and when Morris was identified as the one responsible, some authorities accused him of causing the damage deliberately. In support of this accusation, they pointed to the fact that he had launched the worm not from Cornell but from the Massachusetts Institute of Technology (MIT) to cover his tracks. Ultimately, he was sentenced to three years' probation and four hundred hours of community service and fined more than $10,000. Morris still insists the damage was the result of an unintentional design flaw, and today he is a respected computer expert and a professor at MIT.

interconnections complicates finding solutions because governments have assigned different areas of responsibility to different agencies that historically do not play well with others."[84]

Carr also notes that "there is the matter of political will"[85] to consider, meaning that politicians might not be willing to authorize the money or to take the political risks associated with such an authorization in order to protect against cyberattacks. Other experts have suggested the solution to this problem might be to put the nation's vital computer systems under the control of the military, which could be given a stronger hand in dealing with cyberthreats. But Candace Yu, who has studied this issue for the Truman National Security Project, says, "Some have called for authorizing the military to defend private corporate networks and critical infrastructure sectors, like gas pipelines and water systems. This is unrealistic. The military has neither the specialized expertise nor the capacity to do this; it needs to address only the most urgent threats."[86]

Emphasizing Prevention

Given the complexities involved with apprehending cybercriminals, many experts believe that when it comes to computer security, it is more important to strengthen prevention measures than laws. One way that governments and corporations do this is by employing computer security experts to watch for suspicious activities on computer systems and to uncover security weaknesses in these systems and fix them. Sometimes the experts are former hackers who have turned away from criminal activities. For example, prominent computer security expert Kevin Mitnick was one of the most infamous computer hackers in America when the FBI arrested him in 1995. Mitnick spent five years in prison and three years on supervised probation. Today he has his own company and works with major corporations to help them protect their intellectual property and other sensitive data.

A key tool in providing such protection is the firewall. Firewalls use software or hardware or both to put a virtual wall between a private network or intranet (a certain type of network belonging to an organization) and the world outside the network or intranet. This means that no one without authorization can access what is on one side of the wall from the other. To make sure of this, the firewall evaluates every message entering or leaving the network or intranet and blocks any that are deemed unauthorized.

Any computer user who accesses the Internet should also install reliable antivirus software, which is designed to detect and destroy computer viruses. The website Destroy Adware.com, which helps people prevent and remove adware, spyware, viruses, and other types of malware, says, "If you do not at least have a personal firewall and anti-virus protection then you should not connect your computer to the internet."[87]

The website also advises computer users to take many other precautions as well, such as opening e-mail attachments only after confirming they were sent by a known sender, keeping e-mail addresses confidential and never posting them on an unsecure website, and being wary of downloading and installing programs from the Internet, especially free programs. In addition, the site advises people to type addresses of websites manually rather than using links to go to them, in order to avoid malicious hyperlinks (website links that look like they will take a computer to one site when they are actually linked to another).

Security experts recommend many other precautions as well, including installing operating system updates on a regular basis, choosing secure passwords, not using the same password for every site visited, changing passwords regularly, and educating oneself about all of the security risks facing computer users who access the Internet. However, given how many precautions are necessary and the fact that hackers are continually coming up with new ways to accomplish their goals, even a cautious computer user can still be hacked.

Consequently, security experts also recommend that computer users educate themselves on how to tell that a computer has been hacked. Signs include an unexpected decline in performance, an unexpected increase in file size, unexplained changes to files or network settings, and frequent computer crashes. Busi-

"If you do not at least have a personal firewall and anti-virus protection then you should not connect your computer to the internet."[87]

— Destroy Adware.com, which helps people prevent and remove malware.

ness owners are encouraged to employ people whose job is to monitor computer performance and perhaps to purchase "hacker insurance" as well. This insurance is typically offered by certain companies as part of a broader security management contract. Under this contract, a firm installs and manages a computer security program while insuring against the costs associated with certain types of breaches. Similar insurance policies exist to protect companies from damages caused by fraudulent electronic monetary transactions over the Internet.

An Ethical Problem

Because so much has to be done to keep computers safe from hackers and to mitigate damages if a hacker does strike, some experts say that a better way to address the problem is to make sure hackers understand the ramifications of their actions. Many hackers are

The New York City cybercrime lab (pictured) is just one of many of efforts by law enforcement agencies to combat cybercrime. Some experts warn that the tools of law enforcement are limited and urge public education and awareness as the best defense against hackers.

young people who do not realize the harm they are doing. In fact, some view hacking as laudable. As the website wiseGEEK reports:

> Many hackers are true technology buffs who enjoy learning more about how computers work and consider computer hacking an "art" form. They often enjoy programming and have expert-level skills in one particular program. For these individuals, computer hacking is a real life application of their problem-solving skills. It's a chance to demonstrate their abilities, not an opportunity to harm others.[88]

Cybercrime expert Marc Rogers suggests that some hackers do not see their actions as criminal, because they have no contact with the people or institutions they hack. He explains, "They never see the victims. They never see the impact. All they see is the technology. For the most part, these people understand right and wrong. They wouldn't rob a bank or engage in other deviant criminal activities, but as soon as technology is involved, that line dividing what's right from what's wrong gets really distorted."[89]

Therefore, Rogers sees hacking as something that can truly be prevented only by addressing attitudes. He explains, "If we only rely on law enforcement and the legal system to solve the problem, it's never going to happen. This is a cultural problem. It's an education and awareness problem. It's an ethical problem."[90] Rogers argues that schools should educate kids about computer ethics, but others find his position rather naive. Most hackers, security experts argue, are aware of the ethical issues surrounding hacking but disregard such issues in order to acquire money, influence public policy, and/or to gain prestige in the hacking world.

Facts

- Security experts have determined that when computers are given the task of randomly guessing a person's password, it takes only ten minutes to correctly determine a six-character, all-lowercase password.

- Security experts have determined that a nine-character password that combines lowercase letters, uppercase letters, numbers, and symbols would take a computer 44,530 years to guess.

- The hacker group Anonymous shut down a child pornography site, Lolita City, in 2011 via a DoS attack, then extracted information about its members from the user database and posted it online to aid law enforcement.

- According to its assistant director, A.T. Smith, the Secret Service arrested more than twelve hundred suspected cybercriminals in 2010.

- In 2011 the computer security firm Trusteer reported that in surveying Internet users, it found that 73 percent have the same password for all of their Internet sign-in purposes.

Source Notes

Introduction: Hacking as a Cybercrime

1. Quoted in Jody Barr, "First SC Hacking Victims Come Forward," WISTV News, November 19, 2012. www.wistv.com.

2. Quoted in Barr, "First SC Hacking Victims Come Forward."

3. Brendan Hannigan, "Keeping You Safe: Using Big Data to Secure Big Data," *Huffington Post*, March 20, 2013. www.huffingtonpost.com.

4. Mathew J. Schwartz, "14 Enterprise Security Tips from Anonymous Hacker," *InformationWeek*. August 31, 2011. www.informationweek.com.

5. Peter Ludlow, "What Is a 'Hacktivist'?," *Opinionator* (blog), *New York Times*, January 13, 2013. http://opinionator.blogs.nytimes.com.

6. Quoted in Nicole Perlroth and Evelyn M. Rusli, "Security Start-Ups Catch Fancy of Investors," *New York Times*, August 5, 2012. www.nytimes.com.

Chapter One: What Are the Origins of the Problem of Hacking?

7. David S. Bennahum and Richard Stallman, "Meme 2.04," Into the Matrix, 1996. http://memex.org.

8. Bennahum and Stallman, "Meme 2.04."

9. Richard Stallman, "The Hacker Community and Ethics," GNU Operating System, 2002. www.gnu.org.

10. Stallman, "The Hacker Community and Ethics."

11. Quoted in Associated Press, "Prank Starts 25 Years of Computer Security Woes," CTV News, August 31, 2007. www.ctvnews.ca.

12. Quoted in Ron Rosenbaum, "Secrets of the Little Blue Box," *Slate*, October 7, 2011. www.slate.com.

13. Rosenbaum, "Secrets of the Little Blue Box."

14. Quoted in John Perry Barlow, "Crime and Puzzlement," *Skeptic Tank*, July 1, 1990. www.skeptictank.org.

15. Quoted in Barlow, "Crime and Puzzlement."

16. Quoted in Ene, "A Brief History of Hacking—in the Beginning, There Was MIT . . .," *TechSentry* (blog), June 11, 2011. http://techsentry.wordpress.com /2011/06/11/a-brief-history-of-hacking-in-the-beginning-there-was-mit/.

17. Ene, "A Brief History of Hacking."

18. Quoted in Ene, "A Brief History of Hacking."

Chapter Two: What Damage Can Hacking Do to Individuals?

19. Team GhostShell, Twitter. https://twitter.com.

20. Quoted in *Wired Campus* (blog), "Hacker Group Breaches Thousands of University Records to Protest Higher Education," *Chronicle of Higher Education*, October 3, 2012. http://chronicle.com.

21. Quoted in Julie Xie, "Hackers Leak Personal Info of Students, Employees, and Alums," *Daily Pennsylvanian* (University of Pennsylvania, Philadelphia), October 2, 2012. www.thedp.com.

22. Quoted in Jaikumar Vijayan, "Group Says It Hacked Systems at 100 Major Universities," *Computerworld*, October 3, 2012. www.computerworld.com.

23. Privacy Matters, "Computer Hacking and Identity Theft," 2012. www.privacymatters.com.

24. Memphis Barker, "Think Your Internet Password Is Safe? Think Again . . . ," *Independent* (London), March 8, 2013. www.independent.co.uk.

25. Mat Honan, "How Apple and Amazon Security Flaws Led to My Epic Hacking," *Wired*, August 6, 2012. www.wired.com.

26. Jeremy Schoemaker, "How I Hacked Your Facebook Account," *Shoemoney* (blog), March 8, 2011. www.shoemoney.com.

27. Ramsey, "15 Tips to Stop Facebook & Email Hackers Ruining Your Life," *Blog Tyrant*, June 2011. www.blogtyrant.com.

28. Ramsey, "15 Tips to Stop Facebook & Email Hackers Ruining Your Life."

29. Ramsey, "15 Tips to Stop Facebook & Email Hackers Ruining Your Life."

30. Andy Trask, "Is Your Hacked Email Account Sending Spam to Your Friends?," *Geekablog*, August 25, 2010. www.geekablog.com.

31. Quoted in Matt Liebowitz, "Phishing Gang Steals Victim's Life Savings of $1.6M," NBC News, March 19, 2012. www.nbcnews.com.

32. Quoted in Fiona Roberts, "'Rape of Emotions': Man 'Hacked into Women's Emails and Stole Naked Photos . . . then Posted Them on Their Facebook Pages,'" *Daily Mail* (London), July 21, 2011. www.dailymail.co.uk.

33. Quoted in Greg Risling, "Luis Mijangos Sentenced to 6 Years for 'Sextortion,'" *Huffington Post*, November 1, 2011. www.huffingtonpost.com.

34. Tomer Teller, "Social Engineering: Hacking the Human Mind," *Forbes*, March 29, 2012. www.forbes.com.

Chapter Three: How Does Hacking Harm Businesses?

35. Quoted in Anne Flaherty, "Is Mandiant a 'Digital Blackwater'?," The Big Story, Associated Press, February 21, 2013. http://bigstory/ap.org.

36. Quoted in Ben Elgin, Dune Lawrence, and Michael Riley, "Coke Gets Hacked and Doesn't Tell Anyone," Bloomberg, November 4, 2012. www.bloomberg.com.

37. White House, "Administration Strategy on Mitigating the Theft of U.S. Trade Secrets," February 2013, p. 37. www.whitehouse.gov.

38. Quoted in Michael Riley and Ashlee Vance, "Inside the Chinese Boom in Corporate Espionage," *Bloomberg Businessweek*, March 15, 2012. www.businessweek.com.

39. Quoted in Riley and Vance, "Inside the Chinese Boom in Corporate Espionage."

40. Riley and Vance, "Inside the Chinese Boom in Corporate Espionage."

41. Quoted in Elgin et al., "Coke Gets Hacked and Doesn't Tell Anyone."

42. Nicole Perlroth, "Some Victims of Online Hacking Edge into the Light," *New York Times*, February 20, 2013. www.nytimes.com.

43. Quoted in Diane Bartz and Jim Finkle, "Sony Says 'Anonymous' Set Stage for Data Theft," Reuters, May 4, 2011. www.reuters.com.

44. Quoted in Perlroth, "Some Victims of Online Hacking Edge into the Light."

45. Jeffrey Carr, *Inside Cyber Warfare: Mapping the Cyber Underworld*. Sebastopol, CA: O'Reilly Media, 2012, p. 13.

46. Aaron Weiss, "How to Prevent DoS Attacks," eSecurity Planet, July 2, 2012. www.esecurityplanet.com.

47. Quoted in Amy Carson, "Real Victims, Real Impact, Real Crime," Bright Hub, May 20, 2011. www.brighthub.com.

48. Aaron Weiss, "How to Prevent DoS Attacks."

49. Quoted in Tony Bradley, "Operation Payback: WikiLeaks Avenged by Hacktivists," *PC World*, December 7, 2010. www.pcworld.com.

50. Quoted in Bartz and Finkle, "Sony Says 'Anonymous' Set Stage for Data Theft."

51. Privacy Matters, "Computer Hacking and Identity Theft."

52. Securelist, "Recognizing and Preventing Insider Activity." www.securelist.com.

Chapter Four: How Does Hacking Affect Countries?

53. Quoted in Chris Taylor, "Anonymous Hacks US Government Site, Threatens Supreme 'Warheads,'" *Mashable* (blog), January 25, 2013. http://mashable.com.

54. NoLibya4Syria, "Operation Last Resort," Pastebin, January 30, 2013. http://pastebin.com.

55. Quoted in Taylor Armerding, "Fed Stays Secretive After Anonymous Hack," CSO, February 8, 2013. www.csoonline.com.

56. Gordon M. Snow, "Statement Before the Senate Judiciary Committee, Subcommittee on Crime and Terrorism," FBI, April 12, 2011. www.fbi.gov.

57. Snow, "Statement Before the Senate Judiciary Committee, Subcommittee on Crime and Terrorism."

58. Quoted in Nicole Perlroth, David E. Sanger, and Michael S. Schmidt, "As Hacking Against U.S. Rises, Experts Try to Pin Down Motive," *New York Times*, March 3, 2013. www.nytimes.com.

59. Quoted in Brian Wingfield and Jeff Bliss, "Thousands Could Die If U.S. Power Grid Attacked," *Bloomberg Businessweek*, November 14, 2012. www.businessweek.com.

60. Quoted in Wingfield and Bliss, "Thousands Could Die If U.S. Power Grid Attacked."

61. Quoted in Taylor Armerding, "Department of Energy Hack Exposes Major Vulnerabilities," CSO, February 5, 2013. www.csoonline.com.

62. Quoted in Armerding, "Department of Energy Hack Exposes Major Vulnerabilities."

63. Quoted in Perlroth et al., "As Hacking Against U.S. Rises, Experts Try to Pin Down Motive."

64. Quoted in Nicole Perlroth and Quentin Hardy, "Bank Hacking Was the Work of Iranians, Officials Say," *New York Times*, January 8, 2013. www.nytimes.com.

65. Perlroth and Hardy, "Bank Hacking Was the Work of Iranians, Officials Say."

66. Quoted in Perlroth et al., "As Hacking Against U.S. Rises, Experts Try to Pin Down Motive."

67. Quoted in Perlroth et al., "As Hacking Against U.S. Rises, Experts Try to Pin Down Motive."

68. Quoted in Nick Hopkins, "British Military at Risk of 'Fatal' Cyberattack, MPs Warn," *Guardian* (Manchester, UK), January 8, 2013. www.guardian.co.uk.

69. Kaspersky Lab, "Kaspersky Security Bulletin 2012. Cyber Weapons," SecureList, December 18, 2012. www.securelist.com.

70. Kaspersky Lab, "Kaspersky Security Bulletin 2012."

71. Pierluigi Paganini, "The Rise of Cyber Weapons and Relative Impact on Cyberspace," InfoSec Institute, October 5, 2012. http://resources.infosecinstitute.com.

72. *Economist,* "Getting Ugly," February 23, 2013. www.economist.com.

Chapter Five: Can Hacking Be Prevented?

73. Quoted in Michael Riley and Eric Engleman, "Why Congress Hacked Up a Bill to Stop Hackers," *Bloomberg Businessweek*, November 15, 2012. www.businessweek.com.

74. Riley and Engleman, "Why Congress Hacked Up a Bill to Stop Hackers."

75. Quoted in Riley and Engleman, "Why Congress Hacked Up a Bill to Stop Hackers."

76. Quoted in Dave Smith, "Computer Fraud and Abuse Act 2013: New CFAA Draft Aims to Expand, Not Reform, the 'Worst Law in Technology,'" *International Business Times* (New York, NY), March 28, 2013. www.ibtimes.com.

77. Orin Kerr, "House Judiciary Committee New Draft Bill on Cybersecurity Is Mostly DOJ's Proposed Language from 2011," *The Volokh Conspiracy* (blog), March 25, 2013. www.volokh.com.

78. Quoted in Declan McCullagh, "From 'WarGames' to Aaron Swartz: How U.S. Anti-hacking Law Went Astray," CNET, March 13, 2013. http://news.cnet.com.

79. Quoted in Smith, "Computer Fraud and Abuse Act 2013."

80. Quoted in Grant Gross, "Lawmakers: Tougher Computer Hacking Laws May Be Needed," *Computerworld*, March 13, 2013. www.computerworld.com.

81. Quoted in Meridith Levinson, "Why Law Enforcement Can't Stop Hackers," *CIO*, November 15, 2011. www.cio.com.

82. Quoted in Levinson, "Why Law Enforcement Can't Stop Hackers."

83. Quoted in Perlroth et al., "As Hacking Against U.S. Rises, Experts Try to Pin Down Motive."

84. Carr, *Inside Cyber Warfare*, p. xiii.

85. Carr, *Inside Cyber Warfare*, p. xiii.

86. Quoted in Perlroth et al., "As Hacking Against U.S. Rises, Experts Try to Pin Down Motive."

87. Destroy Adware.com, "Basic Computer Security Tutorial," September 7, 2004. www.destroyadware.com.

88. wiseGEEK, "What Is Computer Hacking?," www.wisegeek.org.

89. Quoted in Levinson, "Why Law Enforcement Can't Stop Hackers."

90. Quoted in Levinson, "Why Law Enforcement Can't Stop Hackers."

Related Organizations and Websites

Anti Virus Information Exchange Network (AVIEN)
website: http://avien.net

An international online community, AVIEN is a network of anti-malware experts throughout the world. These experts share information and efforts in order to reduce the impact of malicious code, including those related to viruses, worms, Trojan horses, and spyware.

Applied Computer Security Associates (ACSA)
2906 Covington Rd.
Silver Spring, MD 20910
e-mail: abrams@acsac.org
website: www.acsac.org/acsa

The ACSA is a nonprofit organization for computer security professionals. It supports activities that seek to improve the field of computer security. Its annual conference brings together security professionals from government, industry, and academia throughout the world to develop solutions to problems related to computer system, network, and information security.

Computer Security Institute (CSI)
350 Hudson St., Suite 300
New York, NY 10014
phone: (610) 604-4604
e-mail: csi@ubm.com
website: http://gocsi.com

Founded in 1974, the Computer Security Institute is an organization for information security professionals. Its main goal is to provide these experts with support, resources, and information related to the field of computer security. To this end, it holds several conferences and events throughout the year and conducts cybercrime-related surveys.

Federal Bureau of Investigations (FBI)

935 Pennsylvania Ave. NW
Washington, DC 20535-0001
phone: (202) 324-3000
Contact page: www.fbi.gov/contact-us
Cybercrime website: www.fbi.gov/about-us/investigate/cyber

The FBI investigates crimes related to more than two hundred types of federal law, including cybercrimes. To this end, the bureau has specially trained cybersquads at FBI headquarters and at each of its fifty-six field offices. It also has cyberaction teams that gather information abroad to help protect national security.

Federal Trade Commission (FTC)

600 Pennsylvania Ave. NW
Washington, DC 20580
phone: (202) 326-2222
Contact page: www.ftc.gov/ftc/contact.shtm
website: www.ftc.gov
Identity Theft website: www.consumer.ftc.gov/features/feature-0014
-identity-theft

The FTC is America's consumer protection agency. To this end, it addresses fraudulent, deceptive, and unfair business practices, including those involving spamming, phishing, identity theft, and other activities related to conducting business online.

Forum of Incident Response and Security Teams (FIRST)

PO Box 1187
Morrisville, NC 27560-1187
e-mail: first-sec@first.org
website: www.first.org

Founded in 1990, FIRST brings together experts on computer security from government, commercial, and academic sectors in order to resolve cybersecurity-related threats. It has dealt with thousands of security vulnerabilities affecting computer systems and networks throughout the world.

High Technology Crime Investigation Association (HTCIA)

3288 Goldstone Dr.
Roseville, CA 95747
phone: (916) 408-1751
e-mail: info@htcia.org
website: www.htcia.org

Growing out of an effort in the mid-1980s to provide law enforcement with the education and training necessary to combat high-tech crime, the HTCIA is an international organization that brings together high-tech specialists for the purpose of supporting and educating them in regard to the prevention, investigation, and prosecution of such crimes.

Identity Theft Resource Center (ITRC)

9672 Via Excelencia
San Diego, CA 92126
phone: (858) 693-7935
e-mail: ITRC@idtheftcenter.org
website: www.idtheftcenter.org

The ITRC provides assistance to victims of identity theft throughout the United States, at no cost to these victims. It also educates consumers, corporations, government agencies, and other organizations on how to protect against and detect fraud and identity theft.

Information Systems Security Association (ISSA)

9220 SW Barbur Blvd. #119-333
Portland, OR 97219
phone: (866) 349-5818
website: www.issa.org

The ISSA is an international organization offering support and education for information-security professionals and practitioners. Its goal is to expand the knowledge of its members and to provide them with opportunities to problem solve. To this end, it offers conferences and publishes a journal with articles related to global cybersecurity.

National Security Institute (NSI)

165 Main St., Suite 215
Medway, MA 02053
phone: (508) 533-9099
e-mail: InfoCtr@nsi.org
website: www.nsi.org

Founded in 1985, the National Security Institute educates defense contractors, government officials, security executives, and leaders of corporations on cyberthreats. It also offers programs to educate employees on how to avoid losing critical information to hackers and other data thieves.

National White Collar Crime Center (NW3C)

10900 Nuckols Rd., Suite 325
Glen Allen, VA 23060
phone: (804) 273-6932
website: www.nw3c.org

The NW3C supports the efforts of law enforcement and regulatory agencies nationwide in preventing, investigating, and prosecuting economic cybercrimes. The organization offers training in computer forensics, cyberinvestigation, and other subjects related to economic and high-tech crime, and its website provides a way for victims to report such crimes.

US Department of Justice (DOJ)

950 Pennsylvania Ave. NW
Washington, DC 20530-0001
phone: (202) 514-2000
e-mail: askdoj@usdoj.gov
website: www.justice.gov

The DOJ is charged with enforcing laws and defending the interests of the United States according to its laws, as well as with ensuring public safety against domestic and foreign threats. It also works to prevent and control crime and to pursue the punishment of people guilty of unlawful behavior, including cybercrimes.

Additional Reading

Books

Kevin Beaver, *Hacking for Dummies.* Hoboken, NJ: Wiley, 2013.

Jeffrey Carr., *Inside Cyber Warfare: Mapping the Cyber Underworld.* Sebastopol, CA: O'Reilly Media, 2012.

Richard A. Clarke and Robert Knake, *Cyber War: The Next Threat to National Security and What to Do About It.* New York: Harper-Collins, 2010.

Christopher Elisan, *Malware, Rootkits & Botnets: A Beginner's Guide.* New York: McGraw-Hill, 2013.

Christopher Hadnagy and Paul Wilson, *Social Engineering: The Art of Human Hacking.* Hoboken, NJ: Wiley, 2010.

Allen Harper, Shon Harris, Jonathan Ness, and Chris Eagle, *Gray Hat Hacking: The Ethical Hackers Handbook.* New York: McGraw-Hill, 2011.

Steven Levy, *Hackers: Heroes of the Computer—25th Anniversary Edition.* Sebastopol, CA: O'Reilly Media, 2010.

Jesse Varsalone, Matthew McFadden, Michael Schearer, Sean Morrissey, and Ben Smith, *Defense Against the Black Arts: How Hackers Do What They Do and How to Protect Against It.* Boca Raton, FL: CRC, 2012.

Steve Weisman, *50 Ways to Protect Your Identity in a Digital Age.* Upper Saddle River, NJ: FT, 2013.

Internet Sources

BBC, "Getting Online One Click at a Time: A Beginner's Guide to Using Computers and the Internet," 2010. http://downloads .bbc.co.uk/connect/BBC_First_Click_Beginners_Guide.pdf.

Paul Gil, "Internet 101: Beginners Quick Reference Guide: A 'Cheat Sheet' for Online Beginners," About.com, April 2013. http://netforbeginners.about.com/od/internet101/tp/Inter net-Beginners-Quick-Reference-Guide.htm.

TopTenz.net, "Top 10 Infamous Hackers," May 24, 2010. www .toptenz.net/top-10-infamous-hackers.php.

Index

Picture Credits

cover: iSockphoto.com

AP Images: 42

© Nicolaus Czarnecki/Zuma Press/Corbis: 54

© Macduff Everton/Corbis: 50

© Colin Matthieu/Hemis/Corbis: 68

© Jared McMillen/Aurora Photos/Corbis: 44

© Christopher Morris/VII/Corbis: 63

© Ramin Talaie/Corbis: 77

Thinkstock Images: 8, 27, 33, 59

© Sion Touhig/Sygma/Corbis: 22

© Nathaniel Welch/Corbis: 14

About the Author

Patricia D. Netzley has written dozens of books for children, teens, and adults. She has also worked as an editor and a writing instructor. She is a member of the Society of Children's Book Writers and Illustrators (SCBWI).